Simply the Best

Simply the Best

FOOD AND WINE FROM

**Kathleen Sloan-McIntosh
and Jenna C. King**

whitecap

Edited by Elaine Jones
Proofread by Lesley Cameron
Cover design by Diane Yee
Typesetting by Diane Yee and Michelle Mayne
Interior design by Warren Clark
Photography by Curtis Trent

Printed and bound in Canada

Library and Archives Canada Cataloguing in Publication

Sloan-McIntosh, Kathleen
        Simply the best : the food and wine from Ontario's finest inns / Kathleen Sloan-McIntosh.

Includes index.
ISBN 1-55285-709-3
ISBN 978-1-55285-709-0

1. Cookery—Ontario. 2. Hotels—Ontario. 3. Bed and breakfast accomodations—Ontario. I. Title.

TX907.5.C22O62 2006   641.5'09713   C2005-906769-1

The publisher acknowledges the support of the Canada Council for the Arts and the Cultural Services Branch of the Government of British Columbia for our publishing program. We acknowledge the financial support of the Government of Canada through the Book Publishing Industry Development Program for our publishing activities.

www.ontariosfinestinns.com
www.ontariosfinestspas.com

The inside pages of this book are 100% recycled, processed chlorine-free paper with 100% post-consumer content. For more information, visit Markets Initiative's website: www.marketsinitiative.org.

Contents

Inn at Christie's Mill

Introduction

They're a peaceful country refuge for the city-worn, a haven for the stressed and weary traveller and simply one of the very best things about Ontario. They may be discovered at the end of a quiet country lane, within a pretty village, next to a placid lake or in the special beauty of Ontario wine country.

They're Ontario's Finest Inns, and throughout the year they keep their promise to travellers to provide the very finest in hospitality and cuisine, luxurious relaxation and a thoroughly unique experience. The inns can be found within an area encompassed by Pelee Island in the west to the environs of Ottawa in the east, south to the Niagara region and as far north as the little village of McKellar—home to the famed Inn at Manitou. Naturally, there's much to discover and experience in each region for each of the four seasons—theatre, art galleries, renowned regional museums, area festivals particular to each area, wineries, restaurants and every sort of recreational sport.

Ontario's Finest Inns is an organization of more than 30 member inns across Ontario, all of which have been judged the finest in their class. Specializing in the best of food, lodging and the fine art of relaxation, each is individual in style and content, offering a unique experience to travellers from across the province, the country and, indeed, the world.

Ontario's Finest Inns provide much more than a place to stay. They offer a sense of time and place unlike other establishments—call it destination accommodation—along with memorable dining experiences featuring the best of regional foods that ensure repeat visits by a faithful following.

Some, like **The Breadalbane Inn** in Fergus, are steeped in architectural history. The Breadalbane is an outstanding example of 1860s Scottish stonemasonry with its ornate ironwork, high ceilings, walnut bannisters and imported marble fireplace.

Others, like the **Domain of Killien** in Haliburton, capture the best of Canadiana in their design. Set in the highlands of Haliburton, the Domain of Killien is situated on a quiet bay amid a 5,000-acre private estate of lakes, forest and rugged hills.

Ste. Anne's Country Inn & Spa, beloved among spa-goers for more than a decade, was recently named one of the world's best spas by British *Vogue* magazine. Another unique member inn is **The Waring House Inn in Picton**. Located in Canada's youngest winery region, Prince Edward County, the inn features an all-season cookery school and presents an array of classes and activities.

Of course, one of the most renowned of the member inns is the **Inn on the Twenty** and the popular restaurant of the same name that originally defined the cuisine of Niagara wine country.

As different and varied as they all are, the commitment to providing fine regional cuisine, whether in the form of a hearty Canadian breakfast or a four-star dining experience, is at the top of each inn's list.

All the inns share the distinction of being unique. As our enviable research has proven to us over and over again, the connecting thread that runs through this tapestry of inns is that no two are alike, each one has its own identifiable style, ambience and characteristics. As if all of this weren't enough to make these inns the great discoveries they are, most also feature the very best of spa treatments in the most nurturing and pampering of environments. Depending on the spa, all manner of wellness programs and services may be included, whether for stress management, yoga, meditation, illness prevention instruction or specialty treatments. These could include massage therapy, therapeutic relaxation, hot stone treatments, reflexology, reiki, organic wraps and facials, hydrotherapy tub treatments, skin care, oxygen treatments, aqua polish, wet sauna and many more diverse applications, as well as classic aesthetic spa services, such as manicures and pedicures. Other inns offer a popular sport or exercise teamed with their spa rejuvenation services, rounding out the experience even more completely.

At a time when "culinary tourism" is a strong factor in the vacationer's decision-making checklist, a guidebook such as this can be an important tool. Not only does it feature the best recipes from each inn, it also profiles the establishments, owners, chefs and culinary brigades that provide some of the most pleasurable dining experiences in the country.

This is our tribute to a very special collection of inns, the wonderful cuisine they provide and the group of seven quality Ontario wineries that generously support and provide the official VQA Ontario wines for the member inns—Pelee Island Winery, Inniskillin, Cave Spring Cellars, Jackson-Triggs, Strewn Winery, Colio Estate Wines and Henry of Pelham Family Estate Winery.

Our grateful thanks to all the inns, the innkeepers, the chefs and the wineries who assisted in the research of this book and who gave of their valuable time. Each one is committed to excellence in hospitality, in dining and in producing the best wine this province has to offer. We hope you will agree that this philosophy is captured within the pages of this book, one part travel and accommodation guide and one part cookbook.

From hearty breakfasts to leisurely lunches, from cocktails and appetizers by the fire to dinner at eight, *Simply the Best: Food and Wine from Ontario's Finest Inns* reveals the culinary secrets of these inns and their chefs. After sampling the recipes, make it your happy mission to visit as many of these Ontario inns as possible—they're ready and waiting and right on our urban doorstep. Enjoy.

Kathleen Sloan-McIntosh
Jenna Claire King

www.ontariosfinestinns.com

Benmiller Inn & Spa

Inn Profiles

Benmiller Inn & Spa

The Benmiller is one of Ontario's most popular and beloved establishments. It could have been called the inn in the hollow, set as it is on a lovely millstream, the Maitland, amid the beauty of Huron County. Comprised of several faithfully restored pioneer woolen mills and mill owners' homes, from the main part of the Inn at the Woolen Mill to Gledhill House, River Mill and Mill House, Benmiller occupies five buildings with a total of 57 unique guest rooms and four private conference rooms.

Authentic mill artifacts are found throughout the property and are used to great effect to add rustic charm to the inn's rooms. Guests may choose from a number of recreational amenities, including the indoor pool, games room, exercise facility or one of many winding nature trails, before enjoying the inn's contemporary full-service spa.

Set in the heart of Ontario's west coast, this region also boasts a strong agricultural heritage as evidenced by the vast farm landscapes that skirt the property. Those farms are also responsible for a variety of foodstuffs that feature on the inn's menu, including rabbit, lamb, game meats, apples, cheeses, the region's bountiful white bean crops and house-made preserves. The gracious, baronial Ivey Dining Room also offers a truly great buffet breakfast that includes local double-smoked bacon and sausages, scrambled eggs with cheese and hefty waffles. An overall patina of comfort and style pervades Benmiller, making it a place to which you will want to return to experience each of the four seasons.

The Breadalbane Inn

Built in 1860 by one of the founders of the historic town of Fergus, today home to the acclaimed annual Fergus Scottish Festival and Highland Games, Breadalbane is owned and operated by the Egger family. Those who appreciate the strength and style of Scottish stonemasonry will be impressed by the inn. The architectural style is carried through to the interior, with soaring ceilings, ornate ironwork, rich walnut bannisters and an imported marble fireplace. Many of the twelve luxurious rooms and suites feature fireplaces and four-poster canopied beds. The beautifully furnished dining room, set in a picturesque curved glass conservatory that looks out over a traditional Victorian garden, is called Maple Shade—the property's original name. Here the emphasis is on fine cuisine with an international influence complemented by a comprehensive VQA (Vintners Quality Alliance) wine list. In fact, innkeeper Peter Egger recently received the Wine Council of Ontario's prestigious award for Breadalbane's impressive collection—and quantity—of fine Ontario wines. The Fergusson Room Pub lists classic Scottish fare on an extensive menu that also includes modern favourites, all prepared by the same culinary brigade who cook for the dining room, and a stellar selection of single malts and local microbrews such as Breadalbane Lager, Hockley Gold Pilsner and three choices from Guelph's renowned F&M Brewery. Breadalbane currently has plans for an inn spa, just one more very good reason to visit.

The Briars Resort & Spa

Family owned, The Briars has been a famous landmark since the 1880s. Fronted by Lake Simcoe, and just a little over an hour from Toronto, The

Briars is set amid stretches of lush lawns, the fragrant cedar hedges for which the area is well known and stately mature trees.

Whether guests stay within the historic Manor House itself, in one of its adjacent wings or at one of the pretty lakeside cottages, there is something for everyone. Golfers will enjoy the 6,300-yard Scottish Woodlands golf course—one of Ontario's finest—while a solarium pool, tennis courts and a quiet private beach are just a few of the recreational facilities available. The Red Barn Theatre, Canada's oldest professional summer theatre, is a short, pleasant walk away. The Summer Dining Room is a beautiful location in which to enjoy casual meals after a day of swimming, strolling by the lake, kayaking, sailing, mountain biking, golfing or reading and relaxing. In the winter months, there are horse-drawn sleigh rides, ice fishing and the opportunity to try your snowshoeing skills. Fine modern country cuisine and a popular Saturday night dinner dance adds to the appeal of The Briars, and the in-house spa completes the picture with massage and aesthetic treatments.

Literary fans will want to visit Sibbald Point, just down the road, and the charming little St. George's Anglican Church where humorist Stephen Leacock and novelist Mazo De La Roche are buried in the graveyard overlooking the lake. Leacock had a particular love of the area. He wrote: "there is a wild grandeur in those Highlands of Scotland, and a majestic solitude where the midnight sun flashes upon the ice peaks of Alaska. But to my thinking, none of those will stand comparison with the smiling beauty of the waters, shores and bays of Lake Simcoe and its sister lake, Couchiching."

The Carmichael Inn & Spa

Built at the turn of the century, and today a designated heritage site, the Carmichael Inn & Spa is an oasis in the heart of bustling Ottawa. With Group of Seven member Franklin Carmichael as its inspiration, the Inn's accommodations explore this group's rich history with a selection of art and biographies.

Each of its 10 rooms are beautifully arranged with a selection of fine antiques. Start your day with fresh-baked muffins, toasted bagels, a selection of cereals and yogurt, fresh-squeezed juices and great coffee served on the wrap-around porch. Guests can enjoy all the capital has to offer—the nearby Rideau Canal, Parliament Hill, the National Arts Centre, the National Gallery, Byward Market and so much more—then visit the Inn's spa for a full range of services before heading out to dine at one of many highly recommended dining spots nearby. Perhaps the most popular option for couples is the Overnight Escape, a great way to unwind and rekindle romance. The package includes overnight accommodation with breakfast and parking, a soothing relaxation massage followed by a couple's herbal bath complemented with music, wine and candles.

The Charles Inn

Named after Charles Richardson, a barrister and Member of Parliament for English Upper Canada who built the house as his residence in 1832, this is considered to be one of the finest examples of Georgian design in Niagara-on-the-Lake, a town with no shortage of impressive architecture. At one point in its history, the lovely old house was purchased from the original owner by Robert Gooderham, son of the founder of Toronto's renowned Gooderham and Worts Distillery. Charles Inn's Four Diamond-awarded dining room is ideal for afternoon tea before the theatre or a sumptuous evening meal prepared by a kitchen headed by one of the region's most talented chefs, Chef William Brunyansky. In the summer months, there are few more pleasurable experiences to compare with a candlelit dinner on the side verandah overlooking the gardens and nearby golf course. There are many reasons to visit the Niagara region, including the Shaw Festival, the many and varied wineries, the famous falls and the countryside itself. The Charles Inn, with its distinctively designed suites, dining room and brilliant menu—one of the best in Niagara—is just one more very appealing reason to add to your list.

Claramount Inn & Spa

During the early twentieth century in Prince Edward County, the historic Colonial Revival dwelling that is home to today's Claramount Inn & Spa was the epicentre of grand society. Today, the County, as it is popularly known, is fast becoming Ontario's newest wine country destination and the Claramount Inn, a gracious country estate overlooking Picton Bay, is once again the centre of attention. Far from the norm, the spa at the Claramount offers time-tested treatments based on the nineteenth-century philosophy of German Sebastian Kneipp, which centre on the therapeutic qualities of water, plants, exercise, nutrition and relaxation. The total inn experience is completed by Clara's, the inn's dining room, with its exceptional wine list and reputation for local, seasonal cuisine, based wherever possible on organic ingredients. The Claramount is the perfect base from which to explore the County and all that it has to offer—charming towns and villages with wonderful little shops and, of course, the many regional wineries.

Domain of Killien

This charming inn sits on a quiet, peaceful bay in Haliburton Highlands. The Domain of Killien, surrounded by a 5,000-acre private estate complete with lakes, forest and rugged hills, is celebrated as much for its situation as for what it has to offer. Whether you choose to stay within the main lodge or one of the lakeside chalets, peace and blissful quiet are yours to experience. A true all-seasons inn, the Domain of Killien offers much for the city-weary—fly-fishing, tennis or a slow paddle on the lake in the summer, crisp cross-country ski trails in winter or the simple magnificence of fall colours. The inn's team of talented French chefs work to create memorable meals, whether it's their signature freshly baked croissants at breakfast or a candlelit dinner, which often feature all-Canadian specialities like salmon and caribou.

Eganridge Inn, Country Club & Spa

The Eganridge Inn is really a combination of two impressive dwellings surrounded by towering pines and acres of meticulously landscaped grounds in the Kawarthas. Think of it as one part century heritage building and one part thoroughly modern country club. The beautifully restored English manor house is on the north shore of sparkling Sturgeon Lake and is often used for weddings and private functions. Nearby, the property's original post-and-beam barn has been revamped and vastly extended to house the warm and inviting pine-panelled dining room, spa and a group of terrace rooms with balconies and patios overlooking the golf course and the lake. Guests can enjoy the challenge of golf on the 3,000-yard, nine-hole woodland golf course and the comforts of an elegant destination spa.

Executive Chef Steve Moghini was born and raised in Switzerland ("the French part") and has cooked at hotels in the Swiss Alps, Tahiti and the Muskokas before coming to Eganridge. His menu features regional cuisine with a modern European style based on local organic produce, where possible, including dairy products and honey, all supplied by local Kawartha operations.

The Elora Mill Inn

It would be difficult to imagine or, indeed, recreate a more naturally beautiful setting for an inn than the one enjoyed by the historic, well-loved Elora Mill Inn.

This renovated gristmill is situated above the thundering falls of the Grand River and the famous Elora Gorge, an awesome setting that, no matter how many times it is experienced, is always impressive. There are dramatic views of the water from many windows—glorious views of the waterfalls and the gorge provide a picturesque backdrop to dinner in the handsome dining room. Exposed beams and stone walls reveal this inn's pedigree as a structure that is over 175 years old. Thanks to the massive walls (over five feet thick at the base), wide window wells provide perfect spots to enjoy a good book. There are year-round special events at the inn, from Robbie Burns night suppers in January through to Thanksgiving and Christmas celebratory dinners. A traditional English tea is served on Sunday afternoons.

Accommodation at the inn is country traditional and thoroughly comfortable. Many of the guest rooms feature fireplaces, jacuzzis or views overlooking the water.

The Gananoque Inn

From its location in the heart of the Thousand Islands, on the banks of the St. Lawrence River, the historic Gananoque Inn has welcomed and served discerning travellers since 1896. Stately guest rooms, some with a fireplace or Jacuzzi, are found in the main inn and adjacent buildings; many of the rooms open onto gardens or river views. The inn's wedding and conference facilities are renowned. Contemporary Canadian cuisine is the hallmark of the dining room, with casual fare on the menu in the inn's popular pub. Both locations offer outdoor riverside dining. Summer activities include golf, kayaking, cycling and river cruises, while winter brings its own special rewards of privacy and seclusion.

The Glenerin Inn

A rambling, stone building reminiscent of an English manor, the Glenerin Inn is located within the greater Toronto area, combining the best of country beauty and urban sophistication. In the 32 guest rooms, accommodations are individually designed for comfort, combining old-world charm with modern conveniences. Fireplaces and private whirlpools add a luxurious touch. Surrounded by landscaped gardens, the Ivor Woodlands and the Sawmill Valley Conservation Area, the Glenerin is a tranquil haven with nature trails just steps from the inn. There are also several excellent golf courses nearby.

Grail Springs Health & Wellness Spa

Inspired by the country estates and castles of Europe, Grail Springs Spa is a visually arresting inn set next to a private spring-fed lake amid hundreds of acres of forests. The moment visitors to the inn approach the massive great oak door, they know they are about to enter an environment that focuses on rest, relaxation and healing. Those who have visited Scotland may recognize that the door is an exact replica of one at the medieval Rosslyn Chapel located just outside of Edinburgh. And the huge stone turret, rich tapestries, torches, wrought-iron detailing and gothic windows do bring to mind another far away time and place.

Since it opened in 1994, Grail Springs has become a destination for those searching for quiet reflection and rejuvenation. Gracious hospitality, casual elegance, fine cuisine and a pristine lakeside setting combine to provide an inspired environment for physical and mental renewal. Accommodation features fireplaces and private baths, and the spa treatments are some of the most diverse and comprehensive offered anywhere in Canada. There are also the fragrant eucalyptus steam room, an outdoor hot tub, modern fitness facilities, a private beach, walking trails, horseback riding and canoeing. In the Great Hall, a room overlooking the lake and gardens, guests can often be found curled up on a down-filled couch next to the stone fireplace, lost in dreams or a good book. And while spa lunches are on the lighter side and geared towards health, guests are invited to splash out a little at the dinner hour and take advantage of the diverse menu that includes fresh local produce and, in season, homegrown herbs and greens from the inn's own gardens.

Harbour House

With a design reminiscent of maritime life in the 1880s, Harbour House beautifully captures the flavour of historic Niagara-on-the-Lake. Hospitality, sensuous comfort and attention to every detail, ensure that guests return again and again. Harbour House is located on a quiet side street overlooking the Niagara River, within easy walking distance of the Shaw Festival and the delights of the Old Town. The 31 guest rooms and suites combine comfort, luxury and up-to-date design, with feather-top beds, sumptuous linens, whirlpool tubs and fireplaces. The staff at Harbour House always manage to make visitors feel a bit like family, offering genuine friendliness and service, qualities that are fast becoming the signature of the Niagara region.

Breakfast is served in the inn's bright conservatory and features fresh baked goods, warm bread puddings and Niagara's bounty of seasonal fresh fruit. If secluded privacy is your choice, you'll want to opt for the Picnic in Your Room, a feature available at the beginning, mid-point or end of the day. Harbour House promotes the award-winning wines of the Niagara region by inviting guests to enjoy a complimentary glass in the lounge during their visits. And, while dinner itself isn't featured, Harbour House invites you to book your evening meal at one of their dining partners in the town and provides a shuttle for this service, just one of the many extras that make this inn so popular.

HighFields Country Inn & Spa

If you're seriously into the spa experience, HighFields is the spot for you. HighFields is a special retreat, tranquil, calm and unhurried—characteristics not unlike those of the owner, Norma Daniels—drawing visitors from all over the world. Just inside the entrance, signed photos of a number of well-known actors and entertainers are featured, as HighFields has long been a destination spa for many in the entertainment world.

Set on 175 acres of rolling hills and woodlands, just one hour north of Toronto, HighFields is a luxurious, ranching-style retreat. Catering to both couples and singles, the inn and spa offer comfortable, personalized accommodation and treatments in a warm atmosphere. The diverse spa menu, which includes massage, body work, facials and hydrotherapy, is drawn from many cultures. Eight guest rooms and suites provide a variety of accommodation styles, while outdoors a swimming pool, tennis court and nature trails beckon.

Meals are taken in a lovely converted century-old barn with its massive stone fireplace and an adjacent screened solarium that is available during the warmer months. Chef Mark Mogensen has had extensive experience in developing menus at a number of prestigious spas and resorts. His dishes are always prepared with local ingredients, organically sourced whenever possible.

The Hillcrest, A Valenova Inn & Spa

Set at the top of the historic town of Port Hope is the Beaux Arts mansion that houses the Hillcrest Spa. Just enough of the new and modern has been embraced, leaving the beautiful old Victorian house to speak of a former elegant era. Prominently placed on a 15-acre estate complete with terraced gardens, woodlands and views of Lake Ontario, the Hillcrest's sumptuous accommodation provides a rejuvenating spa getaway. The emphasis at Hillcrest is strength through wellness, a maxim that is reflected in their company name, Valenova, a hybrid of the Latin *valeo*, a greeting that wishes health, strength and prosperity, and the more familiar *nova*, meaning new. These are themes that are incorporated throughout the array of treatments available like the Dr. Hauschka Detox Program or one of the inn's specialized signature treatments like the Valenova Wave. Especially recommended for yoga followers is the Kundalini Yoga session, offered daily before breakfast to aid digestion.

The twin hallmarks of the Hillcrest are these specialized treatments and the fine health-conscious cuisine designed by Chef Elaina Asselin in her Tuscany-style kitchen—the perfect stress-relieving combination. Tennis and golf facilities are just a short walking distance from the inn and lakefront walks and cycling trails are also close by. The celebrated main street of Port Hope, a leisurely stroll away, offers many interesting shopping opportunities.

Idlewyld Inn

With one elegant foot in the past and the other in the present, the Idlewyld Inn is a gracious retreat in the centre of downtown London. More than 125 years old, the Victorian mansion started life as a private home for a prominent businessman who listed among his credits a position as former mayor of London. The atmosphere of another time and place permeates the rooms and suites at Idlewyld Inn, where contemporary amenities combine with tasteful antique furnishings. The inn serves a buffet breakfast, and throughout the day and evening a selection of juices, coffee, snacks and fresh, house-made sweets are available for guests to enjoy.

The Inn at Christie's Mill

One of the best reasons to visit Ontario's Muskoka Lakes and the region of Georgian Bay is the secluded Inn at Christie's Mill, a four seasons waterfront resort. Visitors are surrounded by stunning views, as the Inn directly overlooks Gloucester Pool and Lock 45 on the well-travelled Trent Severn Waterway. Everything travellers love about this region, including theatres, boating, sightseeing, golf and museums, is virtually on the doorstep. Each of the 30 rooms is stylishly furnished and the spa facility offers a complete range of services including hand and foot care, full massage, body wraps and anti-aging treatments. Twigs is the name of the main lakeside dining room that allows diners to take in the colourful Muskoka sunsets. The menu devised by Executive Chef David Scoffield has a European influence—French in particular—and the chef often returns there for culinary inspiration. During the summer, boaters often choose to conveniently tie up at the inn's dock and head for the spa or the dining room to relax over lunch or dinner.

The Inn at Manitou

Renowned internationally for its elegant professional service and exceptional cuisine, The Inn at Manitou is located on 50 wooded acres along the shores of a beautiful, unspoiled lake. Surrounded by forest and granite, the inn features 34 spacious rooms, most with a lake view. All rooms have a sitting area and fireplace, while luxury rooms feature a sunken lounge, private sauna and whirlpool tub. The inn has a health, fitness and beauty spa, a golf academy and a complete tennis clinic program.

Multilingual, French-born chef Bernard Ibanez has vast experience gleaned from a number of small luxury hotels and resorts. He heads up a talented brigade of 12 international chefs and is responsible for the fine cuisine offered by the inn throughout the day.

Inn at the Falls

Located in the heart of the scenic Muskoka Lakes resort region, Inn at the Falls overlooks Bracebridge Falls and the Muskoka River. Occupying a grand 1870s estate home and six neighbouring houses on a cul-de-sac, Inn at the Falls exudes a quiet village atmosphere. Many of the 42 rooms and suites feature fireplaces, whirlpool tubs, balconies or inviting verandahs.

The inn's Carriage Room dining room has stunning views of Bracebridge Bay and the river, an elegant, romantic atmosphere and a menu centred around continental cuisine created from fresh regional ingredients. The Fox & Hounds, styled after an authentic English pub, features traditional fare and the casual comfort of a log-burning fireplace.

This region is popular in all seasons, and excellent golf, water sports, cross-country skiing, snowmobiling and skating can be found close to the inn.

Inn On The Harbour

Set in the quaint fishing village of Port Stanley, on the north shore of Lake Erie, the Inn on the Harbour blends with nearby wharf buildings in an architectural style reminiscent of a time gone by. The three-storey inn's narrow profile and wooden siding reinforces the established Maritime feeling.

All of the accommodations have a view of the harbour, fireplaces and a distinctive style. Guests can relax on the spacious harbourside deck as fishing boats and pleasure craft drift by or look forward to exploring sandy beaches, boutiques, galleries, restaurants and golf facilities.

Inn On The Harbour offers a continental breakfast of fruit, granola, cereals, locally made baked goods, fresh juice and coffee. For lunch or dinner, choose from a number of restaurants within a short stroll from the inn.

Inn on the Twenty

The acclaimed Inn on the Twenty is in the centre of historic wine country in the village of Jordan. Art, antiques and up-to-date furnishings are unified with an emphasis on comfort. Each suite has a fireplace, whirlpool tub and king-sized bed. The Vintage House, a century-old home adjacent to the Inn, has two guest rooms with queen-sized beds and pine floors.

The inn restaurant, On the Twenty, has been a leader in innovative regional cuisine and a full VQA wine list complements Niagara's bounty of foods. Cave Spring Cellars is on-site and offers daily tastings and tours. In addition to conventional spa treatments, unique vinotherapy treatments are available in the inn's spa located just across the road from the inn proper.

Kettle Creek Inn

Located in a picturesque fishing village on Lake Erie, this 1849 inn is known for exceptional accommodation and outstanding cuisine. The original inn and two custom-built guest houses encircle a quiet courtyard, where English-inspired gardens and a graceful gazebo create a peaceful oasis. The inn's five luxury suites have whirlpools, gas fireplaces, living rooms, private balconies and paintings by local artists.

At the cozy, intimate pub one can unwind with a before-dinner drink before heading into the dining room proper, where the menu always boasts a combination of classic and modern influences and features dishes prepared with local organic ingredients and products such as perch, lamb, venison and rhea.

Nearby are sandy beaches, art galleries and boutiques, the local fitness centre, biking, hiking, sailing and summer theatre.

Lantern Inn

The Lantern Inn is a boutique hotel that anchors Port Hope's Heritage Conservation District and overlooks the Ganaraska River and park. The romance of yesterday blends with the convenience and luxury of today in spacious rooms with high ceilings and well-defined mouldings, a signature feature of the period.

The casual, 1920s Parisian-style dining room offers breakfast, lunch, dinner and a popular brunch on Sundays. Dine by the fire or, during the warmer months, outside on a patio styled after those found in old Montreal. Antique hunters will be happy to learn that the town is reputed to be the antique capital of rural Ontario.

The Little Inn of Bayfield

One of the loveliest reasons to visit Huron County is the charming Heritage Village of Bayfield on the shores of Lake Huron. Here, The Little Inn of Bayfield has been welcoming guests for more than 160 years. A designated heritage building, built of local buff brick, the inn is a fine example of early Ontario architecture. The traditional charm combines with the amenities of today, such as exceptionally comfortable beds with cloud-like duvets, double whirlpools, fireplaces and private verandahs. Throughout the year, the Little Inn offers a series of special events, such as wine and dine dinners, cooking weekends, gardening workshops, birding weekends and more. This all-season inn offers some of the best dining in the region and has received the prestigious *Wine Spectator* magazine's Award of Excellence each year since 1994. The menu is prepared by Chef Jean Jaques Chappuis and his international staff.

A short walk from the inn are the sandy shores of Lake Huron, a great spot for viewing spectacular sunsets. Well-behaved and quiet pets are welcome in the special rooms set aside for those guests travelling with pets.

The Merrill Inn

Built in 1878 for Sir Edwards Merrill, a colleague of Sir John A. Macdonald, this stately inn in the heart of Prince Edward County is surrounded by sweeping, manicured lawns. Owners Amy and Edward Shubert have extensive hospitality experience and a desire to introduce city dwellers in particular to the pleasures of their classic country inn. Their friend, Chef Michael Sullivan, has worked in high-profile Toronto restaurants and takes much pride and joy in crafting a modern menu based on an array of local artisanal ingredients from the county. Like its fellow wine country region, Niagara, Prince Edward County has a bounty of fresh produce with seasonal roadside stands and dining rooms featuring the best of fresh fruits and vegetables. The county's only wine bar is in the inn where you can sample fine wines by the glass from area wineries, locally crafted draft beers and ciders.

The Millcroft Inn & Spa

A high level of luxury and a tranquil location in the rolling Caledon Hills make the Millcroft Inn a peaceful country retreat. Quiet elegance and authentic historic detail provide a balm for the city-weary. Guests enjoy a riverside setting and a hundred acres of thickly wooded trails along with fine cuisine and vintage wines. In addition, the Millcroft Spa, Centre for Well-Being pampers guests with a full range of treatments, including hydrotherapy and massage, aesthetic treatments and fine European products. The Millcroft has many attributes to make your visit memorable, whether you choose to read by the lounge's fragrant wood-burning fireplace after hiking a sun-dappled trail through the woods before dinner or you opt for complete relaxation during one of the many spa treatments available.

Oban Inn & Spa

A Niagara landmark for 170 years, the building that's known as the Oban Inn & Spa continues to welcome guests from across Canada and around the world. Set in the heart of historic Niagara-on-the-Lake, this original country inn overlooks the waters of Lake Ontario and Canada's oldest golf course. Originally built as a private home in 1824 by Captain Duncan Millroy of Oban, Scotland, the original dwelling known as the Oban Inn was devastated by fire on Christmas Day 1992. Happily it was faithfully recreated in every detail to become an exact replica of that original building and reopened near the end of the following year. The "prettiest town in Canada," as Niagara-on-the-Lake is known, offers much to discover, with fine dining, shops, theatre, wineries, all on—or very near—the inn's doorstep. Experience Shaw's Corner Lounge, a favourite with inn dwellers and locals alike, with its cozy, upscale pub environment before, or after, heading in to Kir, the inn's luxurious dining room where the menu features some of the region's finest food.

The Old Mill Inn & Spa

A Toronto landmark for 90 years, The Old Mill Inn is a picturesque English-inspired inn complete with dark, beamed ceilings, fireplaces and its original flagstone flooring. Throughout its illustrious history, the Old Mill has been the place for leisure and recreation, for romance and weddings in its candlelit chapel, anniversaries and more. The inn was a gathering place for Canadian soldiers during World War II and for those who survived the devastation wrought by Hurricane Hazel in 1954. Dining and dancing have been a tradition here since 1921. Surrounded by some of the city's most tranquil parklands along the Humber River and popular for decades for superb dining and traditional afternoon teas, the Old Mill now offers 59 suites with every modern amenity. Guests can unwind and shake off the week's stresses at the Spa at the Old Mill, while the music from live entertainment and a spacious dance floor provide a sophisticated alternative to a conventional night out.

Riverbend Inn & Vineyard

The owners of Niagara's Riverbend Inn & Vineyard, the Wiens family, know a thing or two about running an inn. As the former owners of the Niagara-on-the-Lake property known as the Prince of Wales, they ran the town property with style for 22 years. When they sold it in 1997 they began the search for another place that they could call their own. They found a jewel in the rough when they took possession of the inn now known as the Riverbend, located just outside the town proper, overlooking the Niagara River on the famed Niagara Parkway, in what must surely be one of the province's most dramatic and scenic settings. The inn had been used for a number of other businesses and when the family took it over, it underwent a complete restoration to return it to its original splendour. This is the only Niagara inn situated within a working vineyard, a fact that will thrill wine lovers and those seeking the most original of country settings alike. Seventeen acres of Chardonnay and Merlot vines surround the inn, making the views from rooms and the dining area extra special. Visitors may sip local wines as they relax on the summer patio overlooking the lush vineyards or while they sit comfortably by the fire during the winter months, awaiting a lunch or dinner reservation in the white table-clothed dining room.

Rosemount Inn

This Tuscan-style limestone villa in the city of Kingston, originally built in the 1840s from a design by English-born architect William Coverdale, now has a historic designation. Victorian antiques, linens and lace add gracious accents to guest rooms, each with a private bath. The Coach House, with fireplace, whirlpool tub and loft bedroom, is perfect for a secluded retreat. Massage, aromatherapy and aesthetic treatments in the petite spa are exclusive to guests of the inn.

Gourmet breakfasts are a daily ritual at Rosemount. After dinner at a fine local restaurant and a peaceful night's rest, guests look forward to breakfast in the dining room that includes specialities like Welsh toast with wild blueberries and local maple syrup, apple frittatas with warm brie and toasted walnuts or fresh fruit salad.

Sam Jakes Inn

Just 45 minutes from the bustle of downtown Ottawa, Sam Jakes Inn overlooks the Rideau Canal in historic Merrickville, one of Canada's most beautiful villages. Furnished and decorated in period style, this pretty inn reflects a more tranquil time, making it the perfect urban getaway, wedding location or meeting retreat.

Traditional family hospitality comes naturally to everyone at Sam Jakes, a philosophy that was first establi shed back in 1860. Restored to its original elegance and expanded to become the large country inn it is today, Sam Jakes has a reputation for great local cuisine. Scottish-born Chef Thomas Riding developed his style at a hunting lodge in the Scottish Highlands before heading for Ontario.

Guests may relax in the country gardens or by the fireside in the library lounge, take advantage of the on-site spa, sauna and exercise room or choose to canoe, bike, ski, take a historic walking tour or bird-watch along the Rideau Heritage Route. In the dining room, a full menu includes the finest in local Ontario cuisine, VQA wines, ales and stellar single-malt whiskies. Sunday brunch is a popular choice and, during the summer, guests enjoy live music on the tree-shaded patio.

Sir Sam's Inn & WaterSpa

Haliburton's classic country inn and resort, this lovely old inn sits in a secluded, idyllic setting where nature takes centre stage. Framed by the rolling hills, with Eagle Lake at its door, the inn is Canadiana at its best. A sweeping verandah marks the entrance to the main lodge, a 10-bedroom stone and timber mansion on the shoreline of the lake. The lodge was built by Sir Samuel Hughes, the decorated government minister who led Canada's military through World War II. Today's inn includes 18 lakeside accommodations, a conference wing and a spa. In the heart of Ontario cottage country, guests take advantage of the outdoors in all seasons, whether it's sailing, kayaking, canoeing, mountain biking, downhill or cross-country skiing, snowmobiling or skating. After an active day, they can spend time in the WaterSpa before relaxing by the fire or enjoying a beverage in Gunner's Pub. In the Twin Fires dining room, the gourmet menu is complemented by one of many fine wines from Sir Sam's diminutive wine cellar accessible by a winding cast-iron stairway.

Ste. Anne's Country Inn & Spa

The moment you enter the grounds of this award-winning facility, you know you are in very good hands. Ste. Anne's is a special place that exudes the well-being and comfort exemplified in their motto "bringing the power of healing through human touch to the world." More than 500 acres of rolling hills overlooking Lake Ontario is the peaceful, bucolic setting for Ste. Anne's Country Inn & Spa. It's one of only two Canadian Aveda destination spas and was named one of the top 10 spas in the world by British *Vogue* magazine. Just 75 minutes east of Toronto, the Four Diamond accommodations of the inn include more than a dozen guest suites and an equal number of guest houses, many with fireplace and ensuite bath.

Plans are afoot for a series of developments that will transform this distinguished estate, making it even more of a complete wellness community. The therapeutic benefits offered to visitors through customized spa and fitness programs at Ste. Anne's may be the most significant reason to visit. However, the elegant accommodations, excellent cuisine (prepared exclusively for guests) and attentive staff are also reasons to return.

Trinity House Inn

The award-winning Trinity House Inn has a pedigree dating back to 1859. Located in the heart of the Thousand Islands, famous for its natural beauty and wealth of forest trails and waterways, Trinity House offers superior accommodations, excellence in dining and a warm, inviting atmosphere based on comfortable elegance, as anyone who has relaxed in their sofa lounge or drifted off in the open air rocking chair porch will attest. Selected as Best Canadian Inn in the 2000 Reader's Choice Survey of *North American Country Inn Bed & Breakfast Magazine*, the inn features attractively designed guest rooms decorated with a combination of Victorian eclecticism and contemporary sophistication. Celebrated cuisine with a slight French accent and a wine list that includes a comprehensive selection of VQA wines can be enjoyed by the fireplace or on the pergola and sun terrace overlooking the gardens complete with waterfall. Much fresh fish can be found on the menu in addition to specialties like smoked duck and a wide array of rich, creative desserts.

The Vintage Goose Inn & Spa

The historic and dignified Vintage Goose Inn & Spa dates back to 1877, when it was known as the Wigle O'Heron home. Surrounded by the Lake Erie North Shore wine region, Kingsville, known as the "sun parlour of Canada," is known for its temperate climate, proximity to local wineries and fine sandy beaches.

The inn features a traditional wrap-around porch and carefully tended gardens. Canadiana antiques, gleaming hardwood floors, mahogany trim and leaded glass promote the ambience of yesteryear. Guests at the Vintage Goose Inn may enjoy a variety of spa treatments on the inn grounds.

At the Vintage Goose Restaurant, located just a short walk from the inn proper, local wines and ingredients such as fresh fish and wild game, along with the restaurant's own line of gourmet culinary products, take centre stage on seasonal menus.

The Waring House Inn

Set amid the pastoral beauty of Prince Edward County, The Waring House Inn is a meticulously restored and renovated mid-nineteenth century farmstead whose facilities are enjoyed as much by the locals as by its many visitors from the city. With the County's proud agricultural heritage, it follows that the Waring House is a centre for food-related events. The all-season Cookery School offers a variety of classes and activities, while the Prince Edward Dining Room and the Garden Room menus showcase Canadian regional cuisine. The County, as Prince Edward County is known locally, is fast becoming Canada's newest wine region so, in addition to antiquing, bird-watching, golfing and cycling, guests can enjoy visits to local vineyards, a cidery or brewery.

The Waterloo Hotel

This 1840 Waterloo landmark was initially known as the Farmer's Hotel and later as Bowman House. A few changes in ownership later, in 1904, a new owner changed the name to the Lewis Hotel, described as "traveller's headquarters." Prohibition brought its own influences to bear on the hotel and in 1920 it was purchased by the Royal Bank of Canada, which leased a portion of it to the Waterloo Men's Club, a private establishment where members were often known to enjoy a bit of a tipple "under the table." It wasn't until 1935 that the inn became a proper hotel once again under the name of Waterloo Hotel.

Completely restored in 1997, the Waterloo Hotel has 14 elegant rooms with fireplaces and Canadian antique furnishings. The decor, described as updated Victorian, includes high ceilings, pine floors, rich fabrics and carved walnut beds with feather duvets. A continental breakfast is provided in the European-style café within the hotel, and more than a dozen restaurants—everything from fine dining to bistros and pubs— can be found within a pleasant walk. Adjacent to the hotel is a spa. The

Waterloo Hotel is close to the famous Waterloo County farmers' markets, the village of St. Jacobs and the beauty of the surrounding countryside with its traditional Mennonite communities.

The Westover Inn

The original building, an 1867 limestone Victorian mansion, sits near the banks of the Thames River in the pretty town of St. Marys. During its history, the building was a seminary, and housed an experiment in communal living. In 1987, the inn became as it is today. Situated on 19 landscaped acres, the Westover comprises three buildings that are available to guests. The Manor, the original building, houses the five attractive guest rooms and one luxurious suite. The Terrace, which used to serve as a church dormitory, has 12 guest rooms. The Thames Cottage overlooks the teahouse and lush gardens.

It comes as no surprise to learn that when the renowned actor Christopher Plummer is performing at the Stratford Festival, he chooses to stay at the Westover Inn.

The Westover kitchen is busy throughout the day from morning breakfast to candlelit dinner. Everything served in the restaurant is made at the inn, and that includes breads, jams, ice creams, even the little chocolates left in your room to bid you sweet dreams. Seasonal sports such as golf, tennis, skiing and hiking can be enjoyed close by.

Woodlawn Inn

Originally built in 1835 as a home, the attractive Woodlawn Inn, located in the heart of notable Cobourg, has been welcoming guests since 1988. The quiet, home-like atmosphere of the inn draws visitors from all over the world, and the region alike, and has done since the Della-Casa family expanded their home and converted it to the inn it is today.

The menu at the Woodlawn is inspired in part by the cuisines of northern Italy and southern France. Chef John O'Leary and sous chef Bruce Thorne have created a menu that reflects the seasons, current trends and classic favourites. The inn's well-stocked wine cellar is run by the inn's sommelier, Stephen Della-Casa, who has a firm grounding in the subject of wine and food matching and enjoys sharing his philosophy of fine wine and its ability to enhance the dining experience.

Offering every amenity both for the leisure traveller or corporate executive, with its luxury accommodations and modern meeting facilities, the Woodlawn Inn is an inn for all seasons and all reasons.

Located nearby are broad white beaches, the farmers' market and an array of professional wellness practitioners with day spas, as befits Coburg's title of wellness capital of Canada.

The Lantern Inn

The Breakfast Table

Sunlight streaming through tall windows, lake, forest, vineyard or garden views, tables for two set with gleaming china and fresh flowers, the irresistible aromas of fresh coffee and home baking: these impressions and many more, coupled with warm hospitality, are integral to the experience of breakfast at an Ontario inn. A few inns may offer a buffet-style breakfast with yogurt, fresh fruit, cereals, breads, preserves, muffins, pastries and the like, while others specialize in their unique breakfast offerings. Here are some of the best of both.

Chapter One

THE BREAKFAST TABLE

Marmalade or Apple French Toast

The Idlewyld Inn, London
Makes 8–10 servings

Breakfast at the lovely Victorian Idlewyld Inn includes a number of early morning favourites but perhaps none so welcome as these two creative variations on French toast. Begin preparation for each of these recipes the night before. Both are wonderful with lean sausage or bacon.

Marmalade French Toast

10 slices day-old French bread, cubed
1 cup (250 mL) orange marmalade
1 Tbsp (15 mL) orange juice
5 eggs
½ tsp (2 mL) almond extract
1 cup (250 mL) half-and-half cream
⅔ cup (150 mL) orange juice

Spray the bottom of a round baking dish with non-stick cooking spray. Evenly distribute the bread cubes in the dish. Thin the marmalade with the 1 Tbsp (15 mL) of orange juice and pour over the bread cubes. In a mixing bowl, whisk together the eggs, almond extract, cream and the ⅔ cup (150 mL) of orange juice. Pour this mixture over the bread cubes, partly submerging them. Cover with plastic wrap and refrigerate overnight.

In the morning, preheat the oven to 350°F (180°C). Bake for 35 minutes or until puffed and golden brown and the centre is set. Let sit for about 10 minutes before serving.

Apple French Toast

1 cup (250 mL) packed light brown
   sugar
½ cup (125 mL) butter
2 Tbsp (25 mL) light corn syrup
2 large, tart apples, peeled and sliced
3 eggs
1 cup (250 mL) milk
1 tsp (5 mL) pure vanilla extract
10 slices day-old French bread
1 cup (250 mL) applesauce
1 cup (250 mL) apple jelly
½ tsp (2 mL) ground cinnamon

Combine the brown sugar, butter and corn syrup in a saucepan. Cook for 5 minutes over medium heat, stirring occasionally, until the sugar has completely dissolved and the mixture has come together. Pour into a round medium-sized baking dish. Arrange the apples on top of the mixture.

In a mixing bowl, whisk together the eggs, milk and vanilla. Soak each of the bread slices in the mixture for 1 minute, then place the bread slices over the apples. Pour any remaining liquid over the bread. Cover with plastic wrap and refrigerate overnight.

In the morning, preheat the oven to 350°F (180°C). Bake the French toast for 35 minutes or until puffed and golden brown and the centre is set. While it's baking, combine the applesauce, apple jelly and cinnamon in a small saucepan over medium heat. Whisk the ingredients together until heated through, stirring constantly, about 5 minutes or so. Set to one side and keep warm. Let the French toast stand for 10 minutes before serving with the warm sauce.

Sky-High Savoury Custard

Rosemount Inn, Kingston
Makes 6–8 servings

Rosemount serves a very creative breakfast recipe involving savoury cheese custard squares teamed with oven-dried tomatoes and a mushroom duxelles in phyllo pastry. As wonderful as it is, its preparation is a tad involved for the home chef. Here is a simpler version that uses many of the same ingredients. This calls for regular pastry as the base, but if you are comfortable working with phyllo dough (see Phyllo 101 on page 47) it would work well here, too. Serve immediately or at room temperature with sautéed button mushrooms and cherry tomatoes.

pastry to cover the bottom and sides of a 9-inch (2.5-L) square baking pan

½ lb (250 g) smoked ham, thickly sliced and roughly chopped

3 green onions, trimmed and finely chopped

1 cup (250 mL) shredded aged cheddar cheese

1 cup (250 mL) crumbled chèvre

6 large eggs

¼ tsp (1 mL) salt

1 tsp (5 mL) freshly ground black pepper

1 cup (250 mL) whipping cream

½ cup (125 mL) milk

2 Tbsp (25 mL) chopped fresh parsley

1 tsp (5 mL) chopped fresh thyme

Preheat the oven to 350°F (180°C). Line a 9-inch (2.5-L) square baking pan with pastry, leaving a substantial overhang of about 1 inch (2.5 cm). Scatter ½ the ham, ½ the green onion and ½ of both cheeses over the bottom of the shell.

In a large mixing bowl, blend the eggs well with the salt and pepper. Add the cream, milk, parsley, thyme and remaining ham, onion and cheeses. Blend together well. Place the pastry-lined baking pan on a baking sheet lined with parchment paper or foil. Open the oven door and pull out the rack.

Place the pan on the rack and carefully pour the egg mixture into the pastry shell, slide the rack into the oven and bake for about 50–55 minutes, until it's puffed up and golden brown and a tester inserted in the centre comes out clean. Serve immediately.

Croissant Brunch Soufflé

The Trinity House, Gananoque
Makes 6 servings

A favourite from the Trinity House Inn, this all-in-one dish can easily be assembled the night before and placed in the oven the next morning. This is wonderful with sausages or back bacon and fried tomato halves. Use the large, readily available supermarket croissants for this recipe.

4 day-old croissants, torn into small pieces
½ Spanish onion, minced
2 cups (500 mL) shredded marbled cheese

6 large eggs
1 ¼ cups (300 mL) half-and-half cream
¼ cup (50 mL) grated Parmesan cheese

Lightly spray a glass soufflé dish with cooking spray.

In a large bowl, toss the croissant pieces, onion and grated marbled cheese together. Pack tightly into the glass dish. Combine the eggs and cream in the bowl and whisk together. Pour into the dish; the liquid should just reach the top of the croissant mixture. Sprinkle with the Parmesan cheese. Bake at 325°F (165°C) for 1 ¼ hours. Let stand for 15 minutes before serving.

Fruit, Granola & Lavender Honey Parfait

The Old Mill Inn & Spa, Toronto
Makes 4 servings

You might not necessarily associate breakfast with this traditional English Tudor–style inn, but the first meal of the day is presented with the same attention to detail as every other meal. Vary this recipe by using any seasonal soft fruit in place of the bananas—peaches, plums or nectarines. Start by infusing the honey with the lavender sprigs. If you like, you can use lavender flower honey and omit this step.

½ cup (125 mL) honey
few sprigs fresh lavender
2 cups (500 mL) granola
2 cups (500 mL) assorted fresh
    berries: raspberries, blackberries,
    blueberries or sliced strawberries

1 large banana, sliced
2 cups (500 mL) plain yogurt
4 sprigs fresh mint and 4 whole
    berries for garnish

Combine the honey and lavender in a small, heavy saucepan and cook at a gentle simmer over medium heat for about 5 minutes. Remove from the heat and let cool.

Line up 4 parfait or large martini glasses and assemble the parfait in this fashion: start with a layer of granola in each glass, followed by some fresh berries and sliced banana, then a layer of yogurt and a drizzle of honey. Repeat this twice more for each parfait and end with a final drizzle of honey, a sprig of fresh mint and a berry.

Waterloo County Buttermilk Pancakes

Waterloo Hotel, Waterloo
Makes 4 servings

These old-fashioned and irresistible pancakes are just made to be partnered with pure maple syrup and good-quality pork sausages. Serve with unsalted butter.

2 cups (500 mL) all-purpose flour
1 tsp (5 mL) baking soda
½ tsp (2 mL) salt
1 Tbsp (15 mL) sugar

1 egg
2 cups (500 mL) buttermilk
1 ½ Tbsp (22 mL) canola oil

Preheat the oven to warm. In a large mixing bowl, combine the flour, baking soda, salt and sugar. In a smaller bowl, lightly beat the egg and whisk in the buttermilk and oil. Add to the dry ingredients and mix just until combined; do not overmix.

Set a large, lightly oiled pan (or griddle) over medium-high heat. Ladle the pancake batter into the pan. When small bubbles appear on the surface, flip the pancake over to cook the other side for about 45 seconds. Keep the pancakes warm in the oven while you cook the remaining batter.

Harbour House Homemade Granola

Harbour House Hotel, Niagara-on-the-Lake
Makes about 8 cups (2 L)

Breakfast in the sunny conservatory at Harbour House features one of the best versions of granola we've ever had. Wonderful with plain or flavoured yogurt, sliced bananas, chopped apples, peaches, berries or any fruit combinations you prefer.

2 ½ cups (625 mL) rolled oats
½ cup (125 mL) sliced almonds
½ cup (125 mL) broken walnuts
½ cup (125 mL) chopped pecans
½ cup (125 mL) sesame seeds
½ cup (125 mL) wheat germ
½ cup (125 mL) shredded coconut

½ cup (125 mL) unsalted sunflower seeds
½ cup (125 mL) safflower oil
½ cup (125 mL) honey
½ cup (125 mL) dried cranberries
½ cup (125 mL) raisins
½ cup (125 mL) currants

Preheat the oven to 325°F (160°F). In a very large bowl, place the oats, almonds, walnuts, pecans, sesame seeds, wheat germ, coconut and sunflower seeds. Mix together with your hands to combine well. In a small saucepan, combine the oil and honey over medium heat and warm through, stirring. Pour over the ingredients in the bowl and mix well.

Spread a portion of the mixture onto a baking sheet with sides and bake for about 15 minutes. Stir the mixture around, then bake for a further 15 minutes or until golden brown. Repeat with the remaining mixture. When all the granola is ready and has cooled, pour into the large mixing bowl and stir in the cranberries, raisins and currants. Store in an airtight container for up to 3 weeks.

Apricot & Mascarpone-Stuffed Croissant Toasts

Vintage Goose Inn & Spa, Kingsville
Makes 10–12 servings

This is one of those big recipes that, thanks to its flexible nature, will work quite well when halved. It's a luscious combination of flavours.

7 eggs, lightly beaten
2 cups (500 mL) milk
1 tsp (5 mL) ground cinnamon
1 tsp (5 mL) ground nutmeg
1 cup (250 mL) mascarpone cheese, at room temperature
1 cup (250 mL) cream cheese, at room temperature

1 cup (250 mL) dried apricots (preferably sun-dried), finely chopped
½ cup (125 mL) apricot preserve
12 large croissants, halved
½ cup (125 mL) butter, melted
icing sugar and pure maple syrup to garnish

In a mixing bowl, combine the beaten eggs with the milk, cinnamon and nutmeg until well blended. Pour the mixture into a large shallow dish and set to one side. Wipe the bowl clean. Place the 2 cheeses and apricots in the bowl and blend together. Spread some of this mixture over ½ of each sliced croissant. Spread the apricot preserve over the other ½ and sandwich the croissant together, pressing to seal. Dip each stuffed croissant in the egg and milk mixture, coating thoroughly.

Preheat the oven to warm. Preheat a grill or large pan over medium heat. Use 1 Tbsp (15 mL) of the melted butter to grease the grill or pan. Place one of the croissants on the grill and cook for about 4–5 minutes or until browned on both sides. Transfer to the oven to keep warm while you cook the remaining croissants.

To serve, place a croissant on a warmed plate, dust with a little icing sugar and drizzle with maple syrup.

Orange Popovers

Waterloo Hotel, Waterloo
Makes 12 popovers

This recipe varies a little from the standard popover recipe at the stately Waterloo Hotel, but if you like the original you're bound to go for these. Wonderful served hot with butter and orange marmalade.

¼ cup (50 mL) melted butter
2 cups (500 mL) all-purpose flour
1 tsp (5 mL) salt

4 eggs
2 cups (500 mL) milk
finely grated zest of 1 orange

Preheat the oven to 400°F (200°C). Pour some of the melted butter into each of the 12 cups in a non-stick muffin tin (if using a regular muffin tin, spray with nonstick cooking spray before adding the butter).

Sift the flour and salt into a medium-sized mixing bowl. In another bowl, whisk the eggs together well with a balloon whisk, then whisk in the milk until smooth. Add the flour to the milk and egg mixture, a heaping spoonful at a time, whisking well after each addition. Add the orange zest and whisk once more.

Pour the mixture into a large jug or pitcher and fill each of the muffin tins about ¾ full. Bake on the lowest shelf of your oven for 15–20 minutes. Do not open the oven door. Reduce the temperature to 350°F (180°C) and continue to bake for a further 15–20 minutes until they are golden brown and puffed up. Remove from the oven and serve warm.

Harbour House Blueberry French Toast with Blueberry Orange Sauce

Harbour House Hotel, Niagara-on-the-Lake
Makes 10 servings

Reserve this make-ahead breakfast dish—a Harbour House Hotel favourite—for those times when you have a crowd to feed. A blueberry lover's dream.

For the French toast:

1 ½ cups (375 mL) wild blueberries, fresh or frozen

12 oz (375 g) spreadable cream cheese

18 slices thick-sliced bread

10 eggs

¼ cup (50 mL) pure maple syrup

½ cup (125 mL) melted butter

2 ½ cups (625 mL) half-and-half cream

Spray a 13- × 9-inch (3.5-L) baking dish with non-stick cooking spray and set to one side. In a small mixing bowl, gently fold ½ the blueberries into the cream cheese. Spread this mixture onto 9 of the bread slices. Top each with the remaining slices of bread to form 9 "sandwiches." Using a sharp chef's knife, trim the crusts from all of the sandwiches and cut each into 1-inch (2.5-cm) cubes. Place the cubes in the prepared baking dish. Sprinkle the remaining blueberries over the bread cubes.

In a medium-sized mixing bowl, whisk together the eggs, maple syrup, butter and cream. Pour the mixture over the bread cubes. Cover with plastic wrap and press down slightly so the bread cubes are submerged in the egg mixture. Refrigerate overnight.

When ready to bake, remove from the refrigerator. Preheat the oven to 350°F (180°C). Bake for 40 minutes, or until the top is lightly browned and the centre is set. Meanwhile, make the blueberry orange sauce.

For the blueberry orange sauce:

Makes about 5 cups (1.25 L)

1 ½ cups (375 mL) sugar

1 ½ cups (375 mL) water

¼ cup (50 mL) orange juice

1 ½ tsp (7 mL) grated orange zest

3 Tbsp (45 mL) cornstarch

1 ½ cups (375 mL) wild blueberries,
fresh or frozen

1 ½ Tbsp (22 mL) butter

In a small saucepan over medium-high heat, stir together the sugar, water, juice, zest and cornstarch (use a whisk to prevent lumps). Cook, stirring occasionally, until thickened, about 4–6 minutes. Stir in the blueberries and continue cooking for about 5 more minutes. Add the butter and stir to melt and blend. Serve just warm over servings of blueberry French toast.

Banana Spelt Bread

HighFields Country Inn & Spa, Zephyr
Makes 1 loaf

This nutritious, flavourful breakfast bread features flour made from spelt, an ancient cereal grain high in protein and well tolerated by those with wheat allergies. Look for it in health-food stores. The chef notes that if you use over-ripe bananas that you have stored in the freezer, reduce the amount of water to ¼ cup (50 mL), as the thawed bananas will provide much more liquid.

3 ½ cups (875 mL) whole grain spelt
   flour
½ cup (125 mL) light brown sugar
2 tsp (10 mL) baking powder
1 tsp (5 mL) ground cinnamon
½ tsp (2 mL) allspice

½ tsp (2 mL) salt
1 large egg
2 cups (500 mL) very ripe bananas,
   mashed
½ cup (125 mL) vegetable oil
½ cup (125 mL) water

Preheat the oven to 350°F (180°C). Lightly spray a 9- × 5-inch (2-L) loaf pan with non-stick cooking spray.

In a medium-sized mixing bowl, combine the spelt flour, brown sugar, baking powder, cinnamon, allspice and salt and blend well. In another mixing bowl, whisk the egg and add the bananas, oil and water, blending well together. Gently mix the dry ingredients into the wet mixture until well blended. Do not overmix.

Pour into the prepared loaf pan and bake for about 35–40 minutes until browned and slightly springy to the touch. Transfer to a baking rack to cool.

Hillcrest Spa Breakfast Hash

The Hillcrest, A Valenova Inn & Spa, Port Hope
Makes 2 servings

We enjoyed this colourful dish topped with a poached egg, but it is equally good with scrambled eggs or for dinner where you can team it with grilled fish or roast chicken. As most of the vegetables are cooked ahead of time (or are leftovers) the finished dish does not take long to prepare, making it perfect for breakfast.

1 Tbsp (15 mL) olive oil
2 garlic cloves, roughly chopped
3 cooked potatoes, sliced into rounds
1 red onion, roughly chopped and
    sautéed in 1 Tbsp (15 mL) butter
    until soft and transparent
1 roasted red or yellow bell pepper,
    chopped

½ tsp (2 mL) smoked Hungarian
    paprika
juice of 1 lemon
¼ cup (50 mL) water
3 slim stems asparagus, trimmed and
    cut on the bias
salt and freshly ground black pepper
    to taste

In a frying pan over medium heat, warm the oil and cook the garlic for just a minute. Add the sliced potato and brown on both sides for a few minutes. Add the onion and roasted pepper and stir to combine well. After a minute or two, add the paprika, lemon juice, water and asparagus and stir to mix well into the other ingredients. As soon as the asparagus is tender, remove from the heat. Adjust the seasoning and serve immediately.

Fruit & Nut Loaf

The Hillcrest, A Valenova Inn & Spa, Port Hope
Makes 1 loaf

Moist and nutty, this fruit-filled loaf has no flour and is low in fat. It's quite dense and the lengthy baking time reflects this. Very good with a mid-morning caffe latte.

3 sweet apples, skins on, cored,
    halved and steamed until
    quite soft
2 cups (500 mL) mixed nuts (pecans,
    almonds, walnuts)
1 ½ cups (375 mL) sugar

6 eggs
1 Tbsp (15 mL) grated fresh ginger
1 Tbsp (15 mL) baking powder
½ tsp (2 mL) ground cinnamon
½ cup (125 mL) golden raisins

Lightly spray a 9- × 5-inch (2-L) loaf pan with non-stick cooking spray. Preheat the oven to 375°F (190°C).

In a food processor purée the apples, nuts and sugar into a fine paste. Add the eggs, ginger, baking powder and cinnamon and blend until smooth. Turn the mixture out into a bowl and mix in the raisins. Pour the mixture into the prepared loaf pan and bake for 2 hours or until a tester inserted in the centre comes out clean. Turn out onto a rack to cool.

What-Have-You Croissant Quiche

Rosemount Inn, Kingston
Makes 4 servings

Named for its versatility, this simple and very good recipe makes a great, easy dish for brunch, lunch, breakfast or late-night suppers. It couldn't be easier to pull together and you will love the fact that it may be topped with green onions, sliced tomatoes, sweet peppers, mushrooms, zucchini and any number of cheeses.

2–3 large day-old croissants (use the substantial supermarket croissants)
4 eggs
1 cup (250 mL) milk

3 green onions, finely chopped
1 cup (250 mL) diced tomatoes
½ cup (125 mL) shredded aged cheddar cheese

Lightly spray an 8-inch (20-cm) pie pan with non-stick cooking spray. Halve each of the croissants and arrange in the pie pan to loosely cover the bottom. In a mixing bowl, whisk together the eggs and milk until well blended. Pour this mixture over the croissants. Cover with plastic wrap and leave to soak for an hour or so (or overnight).

When ready to bake, preheat the oven to 350°F (180°C). Remove the plastic wrap and top the croissants with the onion, tomato and shredded cheese scattered evenly over the surface. Bake for about half an hour or until puffed, golden brown and set. Let sit for a few minutes before serving.

Fiesta Egg Scramble Bake

The Vintage Goose Inn & Spa, Kingsville
Makes 8–10 servings

Breakfast at the inn might feature a hearty baked dish like this one that will easily feed a crowd. You can make this recipe in its entirety and refrigerate it, covered. Simply bake it at 350°F (180°C) the following morning.

3 Tbsp (45 mL) olive oil
1 onion, diced
1 garlic clove, finely chopped
2 red bell peppers, seeded and diced
16 eggs
2 cups (500 mL) milk
2 Tbsp (25 mL) Cajun or Creole spice
    mixture (look for Louisiana Chef
    Paul Prudhomme's seasonings
    in the spice section of your
    supermarket) or barbecue
    seasoning

salt and freshly ground black pepper
    to taste
three 12-inch (30-cm) flour tortillas
4 tomatoes, sliced
1 lb (500 g) lean cooked ham, diced
½ lb (250 g) aged cheddar cheese,
    shredded

In a large frying pan, warm 2 Tbsp (25 mL) of the oil over medium-high heat. Add the onion and garlic and sauté for a few minutes, then add the bell peppers and continue to sauté for about 6 minutes until the vegetables are softened. Set to one side.

Break the eggs into a large mixing bowl (or the bowl of an electric mixer) and whisk together, then add the milk and whisk until well blended. Whisk in the spice mixture and season with salt and pepper. In a large, non-stick frying pan, warm the remaining oil over medium-high heat and add the egg mixture. Scramble the eggs using a wooden spatula or spoon. Just before they are completely cooked, add the reserved onion and pepper mixture, stirring it well into the eggs. Remove from the heat. Preheat the oven to 350°F (180°C).

Spray a 13- × 9-inch (3.5-L) baking dish with non-stick cooking spray. Lay 1 tortilla on the bottom and add a layer of the scrambled egg mixture over it followed by a few sliced tomatoes, a portion of the diced ham and a sprinkling of cheese. Repeat this process with the remaining tortillas and filling ingredients, ending with the cheese. Bake in the preheated oven for 35–45 minutes, at which point the cheese should be melted and golden brown and the centre of the dish hot. Remove from the oven and let sit for a few minutes before serving.

Phyllo Breakfast Pizza

Sir Sam's Inn & WaterSpa, Haliburton
Makes 8–10 servings

Among the interesting offerings on a menu that changes with the seasons at Sir Sam's is a puff pastry tart topped with cheese, bacon and tomatoes. We think the chef at Sir Sam's will like this spin on his original recipe. You will be amazed at how well this works as a breakfast or brunch dish, especially when sided with scrambled eggs or sausage or both.

5 Tbsp (75 mL) butter, melted, kept warm

seven 17- × 12-inch (40- × 30-cm) sheets of phyllo, stacked between 2 sheets of wax paper and covered with a damp tea towel

½ cup (125 mL) freshly grated Parmesan cheese

1 cup (250 mL) shredded mozzarella cheese

1 cup (250 mL) very thinly sliced onion

2 lb (1 kg) tomatoes (about 5) cut into ¼-inch (5-mm) thick slices

½ tsp (2 mL) dried oregano, crumbled

½ tsp (2 mL) dried basil, crumbled

½ tsp (2 mL) dried thyme, crumbled

¼ cup (50 mL) olive oil

Preheat the oven to 375°F (190°C). Brush a baking sheet lightly with some of the butter, lay 1 sheet of the phyllo on the baking sheet and brush it lightly with butter. Sprinkle the phyllo with some of the Parmesan, place another sheet of phyllo on top and press it firmly so that it adheres to the bottom layer. Repeat this with the remaining phyllo, brushing each sheet with butter and sprinkling with Parmesan (reserve 1 Tbsp/15 mL of Parmesan). When all the phyllo has been used, sprinkle the top with mozzarella, scatter the onion evenly over the cheese, than arrange the tomatoes in a layer over the surface. Sprinkle with the remaining Tbsp (15 mL) of Parmesan and scatter the crumbled herbs over all, adding a little salt and freshly ground black pepper if you like. Drizzle with olive oil.

Bake in the preheated oven for 30–35 minutes or until the edges are golden and crisp. Remove from the oven and let sit for 10 minutes or so before cutting with a pizza wheel or kitchen shears into squares.

Phyllo 101: Like choux pastry and croissant dough, phyllo suffers from a bad rap. It's said to be difficult to work with, and to be temperamental and susceptible to no end of weather- and humidity-related problems. While it is true that a very hot and dry day will accelerate the dough drying out—anathema to phyllo—phyllo is actually the most easygoing and pliant of pastry doughs, making very few demands on the part of the home cook. It's even kind to novice bakers and cooks, allowing itself to be gathered, scrunched, layered, stacked, cut, folded, used to line muffin cups, baking pans and pie plates or used in its entirety to elegantly encase a sumptuous wheel of Brie before baking. And if you have never used phyllo to enclose a delicate piece of salmon treated to a little butter and dill, we don't know what you are waiting for.

But there are a handful of things that will facilitate your time with frozen phyllo dough and they should be heeded. Allow enough time for the dough to thaw in the refrigerator (usually overnight). Then, let it sit at room temperature for about 2 hours or so before using it. If you are not using the entire package, remove the sheets you require for your recipe and carefully reroll the rest, replace the plastic wrap and store in the refrigerator. You should plan to use the remaining dough within the month. Use a damp cloth to cover the unused dough as you work. Phyllo sheets need a thin application of melted butter—we think unsalted is best.

Get-Up-&-Go Muffins

Carmichael Inn & Spa, Ottawa
Makes 12 muffins

Brian Fewster of the Carmichael Inn & Spa in Ottawa says "most of our guests are get-up-and-go people, so we provide a get-up-and-go breakfast, consisting of granola, yogurt, bagels, fresh fruit and juices, home-baked muffins and, of course, great coffee. We bake fresh muffins every morning and each one has a wonderful, distinct aroma. In fact, our regulars, upon wakening, know which muffin is baking because the aroma permeates the entire inn. When it is their favourite muffin, they know they are in for a great day." These delightful muffins are guaranteed to get any day off to a great start.

For the streusel nut topping:

½ cup (125 mL) firmly packed dark brown sugar

¼ cup (50 mL) all-purpose flour

1 ½ tsp (7 mL) finely grated lemon or orange zest

¾ cup (175 mL) chopped, toasted pecans (or walnuts), cooled completely

¼ cup (50 mL) melted butter

Preheat the oven to 375°F (190°C). Spray a 12-cup muffin pan with non-stick cooking spray (or lightly butter) and then line the pan with paper baking cups.

In a small mixing bowl, combine the brown sugar, flour and lemon or orange zest together. Add the toasted nuts and melted butter and stir to combine. Set to one side.

For the muffin batter:

1 ½ cups (375 mL) all-purpose flour

½ cup (125 mL) firmly packed dark
brown sugar

¼ cup (50 mL) granulated sugar

2 tsp (10 mL) baking powder

1 ½ tsp (7 mL) finely grated lemon or
orange zest

1 tsp (5 mL) ground cinnamon

¼ tsp (1 mL) salt

½ cup (125 mL) milk

½ cup (125 mL) melted, cooled butter

2 eggs, lightly beaten

1 ½ cups (375 mL) frozen blueberries
or raspberries, thawed and
drained

¼ cup (50 mL) all-purpose flour

In a large mixing bowl, combine the 1 ½ cups (375 mL) flour, sugars, baking powder, lemon or orange zest, cinnamon and salt and mix well. Make a well in the centre of the dry ingredients. In another small bowl, whisk together the milk, melted butter and eggs. Pour this mixture into the dry ingredients, mixing until relatively smooth. In the same small bowl, toss the thawed berries together with the ¼ cup (50 mL) flour until well-coated. Carefully fold the berries into the batter until well incorporated, then spoon the batter into the muffin cups. Top each with a heaping table-spoon (15 mL) of the streusel nut mixture. Bake for about 25–30 minutes until a tester inserted in the centre comes out clean. Cool for 10 minutes then turn out onto a rack. Serve warm.

Rosemount Inn Welsh Toast

Rosemount Inn, Kingston
Makes 6 servings

This fragrant dish features orange liqueur, orange zest and freshly ground nutmeg. At the Rosemount they like to serve it with whipped cream, fresh berries and a bit of orange zest or mint leaves for a garnish. This is another preparation that can sit overnight in the refrigerator.

1 loaf egg bread, sliced into 1-inch
   (2.5-cm) slices (9 slices)
4 eggs, plus 2 egg whites
½ cup (125mL) sugar
¼ tsp (1 mL) salt

3 cups (750 mL) milk
1 Tbsp (15 mL) Grand Marnier or Triple
   Sec
grated zest of 1 orange
1 tsp (5 mL) freshly grated nutmeg

Arrange the bread slices on a large baking pan or sheet (with sides). In a mixing bowl, whisk together the eggs, egg whites, sugar, salt, milk, liqueur and orange zest. Pour this mixture over the bread, making sure each slice is saturated with the liquid. Cover and let stand 1 hour or refrigerate overnight.

When ready to complete the dish, preheat the oven to 400°F (200°C). On a lightly oiled griddle, brown both sides of the bread slices, transferring them to a non-stick baking sheet as you work. When all the slices have been browned, bake for 20 minutes. To serve, slice each piece of bread in ½ on an angle. Place 3 overlapping slices on a plate and drizzle with warmed maple syrup or serve as described above.

Gazpacho Cocktail

The Vintage Goose Inn & Spa, Kingsville
Makes 4 servings

Enjoy this vibrant beverage as a brunch accompaniment, or use it as a little hair-of-the-dog potion—it will work very well either way. Adjust the hot pepper seasoning to taste. You'll need a blender or food processor for this recipe.

2 Tbsp (25 mL) fresh lemon juice
2 roasted red bell peppers, seeded
   and roughly chopped
¼ sweet white onion (like Vidalia),
   roughly chopped
¼ fresh jalapeño pepper, seeded and
   roughly chopped, or a few dashes
   hot pepper sauce

2 cups (500 mL) tomato juice
½ tsp (2 mL) ground black pepper
1 Tbsp (15 mL) horseradish (fresh or
   jarred)
½ cup (125 mL) vodka (regular or
   infused with lemon or hot pepper)
4 green onions, trimmed and green
   ends feathered

In a food processor or blender, combine the lemon juice, bell peppers, onion and jalapeño and process just until blended. Add the tomato juice about ½ cup (125 mL) at a time, pulsing once or twice after each addition, until blended. Stir in the black pepper, horseradish and vodka. Pour into tall glasses over ice cubes and garnish each with a green onion.

Three-Egg Frittata

Sam Jakes Inn, Merrickville
Makes 2 servings

Because much of the preparation is done ahead of time, this may be the quickest method ever for cooking this Italian-style omelet. At the inn, they like to serve this with "Mrs. McGarrigle's Fresh Tomato Relish." Chili sauce, chutney or even store-bought salsa would work well, too. You will need an 8-inch (20-cm) frying pan for this.

1 Tbsp (15 mL) butter
1 farmer's sausage, cooked and
  crumbled
2 slices bacon, cooked and chopped
1 potato, cooked and chopped
5 cherry tomatoes

3 eggs
2 Tbsp (25 mL) cream
2 oz (50 g) aged cheddar cheese,
  shredded
salt and freshly ground black pepper
  to taste

Preheat the oven broiler. Melt the butter in a frying pan over medium heat. Scatter the cooked sausage, bacon, potato and cherry tomatoes into the pan, stirring to combine. Whisk the eggs together with the cream in a small mixing bowl and add the cheddar. Season with salt and pepper, whisk again and then add to the mixture in the frying pan. When it is partially set, gently run a narrow spatula around the edges of the pan to lift the cooked egg up and allow any uncooked egg mixture to run beneath; cook for 5 minutes or so until the frittata is cooked on the bottom and is almost set.

Place the frying pan beneath the broiler. Cook for 1 to 2 minutes or until the top is set and golden brown. Serve immediately.

Small Seasonal Firsts
Bowls & Plates

Perhaps more than their city counterparts, the well-rounded menus of Ontario country inns reflect the four seasons. Nowhere is this more evident than in the vibrant soups, salads and creative appetizers in this chapter, which includes seasonal first course items to be enjoyed at the appropriate time of year. You'll find butternut squash and pumpkin soups for fall, bright green asparagus soup for spring, summery salads featuring all manner of greens and grains, and other small plate items that work for appetizers, lunch or late-night noshing.

Chapter Two

SMALL SEASONAL FIRSTS—BOWLS & PLATES

Lake Huron Smoked Wild Lake Trout Spread

The Little Inn of Bayfield, Bayfield
Recommended: Cave Spring Cellars Chardonnay Musqué
Makes 6 servings

At the Little Inn, they're renowned for treating the succulent Lake Huron trout to a cure involving salt, brown sugar, fresh dill and fennel seeds before cold-smoking the fish. Not everyone has access to a cold smoker, so this variation calls for 12 oz (375 g) of smoked trout fillets. Smoke them yourself or pick up the fillets at your local fishmonger. Serve with bread that has been rubbed with garlic and brushed with olive oil before grilling, or as the star attraction with a colourful plate of crudités. A thin layer of melted butter will allow the spread to keep for 2–3 days in the refrigerator.

12 oz (350 g) smoked trout fillets, skin removed
½ cup (125 mL) sour cream
½ cup (125 mL) farmer's cheese or dry cottage cheese
2 Tbsp (25 mL) lemon juice
pinch cayenne
salt and freshly ground white pepper to taste

In a food processor, purée the fish fillets. Add the sour cream and cheese; blend until smooth. Add the lemon juice, cayenne, salt and pepper. Process until just combined.

Pour into ramekins and cover with plastic wrap. Chill for up to 3 hours.

Roasted Pumpkin Soup
with Maple Crème Fraîche

The Kettle Creek Inn, Port Stanley
Recommended: Strewn Winery Riesling-Gewurtztraminer Semi-Dry
Makes 6 servings

Here is one of the daily soups served at the Kettle Creek Inn during fall and winter months. Reserve some of the pumpkin seeds to toast for a garnish. Note that the maple crème fraîche should be made a day in advance.

For the maple crème fraîche:
2 cups (500 mL) whipping cream

2 Tbsp (25 mL) buttermilk

¼ cup (50 mL) maple syrup

Combine the cream and buttermilk in a large glass jar. Loosely cover and leave in a warm place overnight (the top of the refrigerator is ideal). The next day, stir well and refrigerate. Add the maple syrup once the mixture is cold and thickened.

For the soup:
2 lb (1 kg) pumpkin (use the small sugar pumpkins), peeled and cut into large pieces

3 Tbsp (45 mL) olive oil

1 Tbsp (15 mL) butter, melted

1 tsp (5 mL) salt

1 tsp (5 mL) freshly ground black pepper

4 cups (1 L) chicken stock

1 large onion, finely chopped

1 bay leaf

½ tsp (2.5 mL) white pepper

pinch each ground cinnamon and nutmeg

½ cup (125 mL) whipping cream

Preheat the oven to 425°F (220°C). Place the pumpkin pieces in a roasting pan and toss with the oil, butter, salt and black pepper. Roast, tossing the pieces often, for about 15 or 20 minutes or until it is beginning to colour. (It does not have to be cooked through as it will cook further in the stock.) Transfer the pieces to a large soup pot and add the chicken stock, onion, bay leaf, white pepper, cinnamon and nutmeg. Bring to a boil, reduce the heat and simmer for about 20 minutes or until the vegetables are fully softened. Use a hand-held immersion blender to purée the mixture until smooth. Continue to purée the mixture while adding the cream. Adjust the seasoning. Serve hot with a dollop of maple crème fraîche.

Harvest Butternut Squash Soup

The Old Mill Inn & Spa
Recommended: Hillebrand Chardonnay, Glenlake Vineyard
Makes 4–6 servings

This classic soup is perfect for fall or early winter dinners and is easily made the day before and reheated when needed.

1 ½ lb (750 g) butternut squash, peeled and cut into large pieces

3 Tbsp (45 mL) olive oil

salt and freshly ground black pepper to taste

1 Tbsp (15 mL) butter

1 onion, finely chopped

1 large leek, white part only, finely chopped

1 tsp (5 mL) ground cumin

1 tsp (5 mL) fresh ginger, peeled and minced

4 cups (1 L) chicken stock, fresh or canned

1 Yukon Gold potato, peeled and chopped

1 bay leaf

1 sprig fresh thyme

¼ cup (50 mL) whipping cream

Preheat the oven to 425°F (220°C). Toss the squash with 2 Tbsp (25 mL) of the oil. Season with salt and pepper and roast in a pan for about 30–40 minutes or until lightly browned. Remove from the oven and let cool.

Place a sauté pan over medium-high heat and add the remaining oil and the butter. Add the onion and leek and sauté until softened. Add the cumin and ginger and continue cooking for about 5 minutes. Remove from the heat.

Place the chicken stock in a large saucepan and bring to a gentle boil. Add the squash, onion and leek mixture and chopped potato to the saucepan. Add the bay leaf and thyme and simmer until the potato is soft and beginning to fall apart, about 10 minutes or so.

Remove the bay leaf and thyme. Transfer the soup to a blender or food processor and process until a smooth and lightly thickened consistency is achieved. Wipe the saucepan clean and return the soup to it. Add the cream, adjust the seasoning and reheat very gently.

Hillebrand Estates Winery

Located in the heart of Niagara-on-the-Lake's wine region, Hillebrand Estates works closely with local growers to produce wines with a "regional taste." Boasting a series of wines, including Vineyard Select, Collector's Choice and Harvest Collections, Hillebrand has received over 300 awards since its founding in 1982.

The winery also features one of the region's loveliest dining rooms with vineyard views. Regional cuisine has long been the focus of chef Tony de Luca's menu at Hillebrand Vineyard Café, thanks to his knowledge of local growers and producers, many of whom are brought to his attention by forager John Laidman. The winery features daily winery tours and events like Springtime in the Vineyard—a guided viticulture tour of the Stone Road Vineyard—as well as two popular jazz and blues concerts in July and August

Bisque de Homard—Lobster Bisque

The Charles Inn, Niagara-on-the-Lake
Recommended: Pelee Island Winery Vinedresser Series Chardonnay Barrique
Makes 4–6 servings

The best and most intensely flavoured lobster bisque we have ever enjoyed was created by Chef William Brunyansky at the Charles Inn, and it inspires this version. Somehow, this luxurious first course tastes even more of fresh lobster than, well, fresh lobster, because the shell of the lobster is used to make the stock, resulting in a deep, rich flavour. If you can obtain a hen lobster, the red coral (roe) will give it even more intense colour. Because it is so luxurious, a little of this lustrous soup goes a long way.

1 ½-lb (750-g) cooked lobster
4 cups (1 L) water
1 medium onion, finely chopped
¼ fennel bulb, finely chopped
1 medium carrot, finely chopped
1 large ripe tomato, chopped
2 fresh parsley sprigs
2 thyme sprigs
1 bay leaf
4 thin slices fresh ginger

salt and freshly ground white pepper
to taste
¾ cup (175 mL) dry white wine
¼ cup (50 mL) cognac or brandy
3 Tbsp (45 mL) butter
¼ cup (50 mL) all-purpose flour
1 cup (250 mL) whipping cream
4 Tbsp (60 mL) finely chopped fennel
fronds

Remove all the flesh and coral from the lobster. Place in a bowl and set to one side. Remove the tomalley (liver) and discard. (Or use it to enrich the stock if you prefer.)

Crush the lobster shells with a sharp knife and place in a large saucepan with the water, onion, fennel bulb, carrot, tomato, parsley, thyme, bay leaf, ginger, salt and pepper, wine and cognac or brandy. Cover and bring to a boil over high heat, then reduce the temperature and allow the mixture to simmer for 30 minutes. As it is simmering, finely chop the lobster meat (some chefs pound the meat to a sort of paste) and reserve.

Strain the stock through a sieve into a bowl. Wipe the saucepan clean and heat the butter in it over medium-high heat. When it has melted, whisk in the flour and cook, stirring, for 2–3 minutes. Add the lobster stock, whisking as you do so, and bring to a boil. Stir until the mixture has thickened. Add the lobster meat (and coral if using) and cream to the mixture. Heat gently, adjust the seasoning and serve garnished with fennel fronds.

Roasted Plum Tomato Bisque

The Trinity House Inn, Gananoque
Recommended: Colio Estate Wines Cabernet Franc
Makes 6–8 servings

This is the definitive fresh tomato soup. The chef likes to serve this with house-made herb croutons.

12 ripe plum tomatoes
2 Tbsp (25 mL) olive oil
4 Tbsp (60 mL) unsalted butter
1 Tbsp (15 mL) finely chopped bacon
1 Spanish onion, chopped
1 carrot, chopped
1 celery stalk, chopped
4 garlic cloves, minced
5 Tbsp (75 mL) all-purpose flour

5 cups (1.25 L) chicken stock (if using
    canned, choose low-salt version)
3 fresh parsley sprigs
3 fresh thyme sprigs
1 bay leaf
1 ¾ tsp (9 mL) kosher salt
freshly ground black pepper to taste
1 cup (250 mL) whipping cream

Preheat the oven to 350°F (180°C). Place the plum tomatoes on a baking pan and drizzle with olive oil. Bake in the oven until they have collapsed and are beginning to char.

Heat the butter in a large soup pot over medium-high heat. Add the bacon and sauté until crisp and most of the fat has been rendered, about 1 minute. Use a slotted spoon to transfer the bacon to a plate and set aside. Add the onion, carrot, celery and garlic to the fat in the pot and cook, covered, stirring occasionally, until soft and fragrant, about 8 minutes. Stir in the flour and cook, stirring, for 3 minutes. Pour in the broth; as the mixture comes to a boil, whisk to prevent lumps. Add the roasted tomatoes to the pot.

Tie the parsley, thyme and bay leaf (bouquet garni) together with kitchen twine and add to the pot. Lower the heat to allow the mixture to simmer for 30 minutes. Allow to cool. When mixture has cooled, remove and discard the bouquet garni.

Working in batches, transfer the mixture to a blender or food processor and purée until smooth. Place a sieve over a large bowl and pour the puréed mixture through the sieve, rubbing the mixture against the sides of the sieve to get as much as possible through the sieve into the bowl. Scrape the undersides of the sieve with a spatula. Wipe the soup pot clean and return the soup to it. Reheat over medium heat. Season with salt and pepper. When ready to serve, whisk the whipping cream until thickened and floppy. Place a dollop in each serving bowl and surround the cream with the tomato soup. Serve immediately.

Baked Maple-Glazed Pumpkin & Pear Soup

Eganridge Inn, Country Club & Spa, Fenelon Falls
Recommended: Cave Spring Cellars Off Dry Riesling
Makes 8 servings

Chef Steve Moghini likes to serve this soup with a golden-brown cover of puff pastry. Readily available frozen puff pastry may be used to add this crowning touch. Use your ovenproof soup cup or bowl as a template when cutting out the pastry so that it will be the correct size. However, Chef Moghini says this soup is also delicious without the pastry. Simply garnish with toasted pumpkin seeds or toasted almonds.

2 Tbsp (25 mL) butter
1 small carrot, chopped
1 small onion, chopped
2 pears, peeled, cored and chopped
1 sweet potato, peeled and chopped
3 lb (1.5 kg) sugar pumpkin, peeled,
    seeded and chopped
¼ cup (50 mL) pure maple syrup

6 cups (1.5 L) chicken stock
1 cup (250 mL) milk
salt and freshly ground black pepper
    to taste
17-oz (500 g) package of puff pastry,
    thawed and unbaked
1 egg, lightly beaten with ¼ cup
    (50 mL) water

In a large soup pot, melt the butter over medium-high heat. Sauté the carrot and onion in the butter until the onion is transparent, about 5 minutes or so. Add the pears, sweet potato and pumpkin, stir to combine well, then pour the maple syrup over the vegetables. Stir together for 2–3 minutes to glaze the vegetables. Add the chicken stock and bring the mixture to a boil. Reduce the heat to a gentle boil and cook the soup for about an hour.

Add the milk and stir to combine. Allow to cool slightly, then purée the soup in a blender or food processor, working in batches. Season with salt and pepper.

Preheat the oven to 400°F (200°C). Assemble 8 ovenproof soup cups and cut circles of puff pastry large enough to cover each. Pour the soup into each of the cups. Using a pastry brush, brush the pastry circles on both sides with the egg wash. Place over each cup of soup.

Bake the soup for about 10 minutes or until the pastry is puffed up and golden brown. Serve immediately.

French Vegetable Soup with Pistou

HighFields Country Inn & Spa, Zephyr
Recommended: Jackson-Triggs Proprietor's Selection Sauvignon Blanc
Makes 4–6 servings

Very similar to Italian minestrone, this hearty vegetable soup is finished with the classic French version of pesto (pistou)—fresh basil pounded with garlic, olive oil and Parmesan. The brilliant green paste is added to a bowl of the soup a moment before serving. As good as it is in this soup, you will also want to use pistou to dress cooked pasta, or as a topping for pan-seared fish fillets or chicken breasts. You can make pistou in a food processor or blender, if you must, but you will achieve more authentic results (and revel in the wonderful fragrances) if you make it by hand with a pestle and mortar. The resulting pistou may be covered and stored in the refrigerator for a day or frozen for up to 6 months. If frozen, bring to room temperature and give it a good stir before using.

For the soup:

1 ½ cups (375 mL) dried small white kidney beans (also known as cannellini) or navy beans, soaked overnight in water to cover, then drained

¼ cup (50 mL) olive oil

3 garlic cloves, finely chopped

2 celery stalks, trimmed and finely chopped

1 onion, finely chopped

2 carrots, finely chopped

6 cups (1.5 L) chicken broth

2 Tbsp (25 mL) tomato paste

½ small head (about 6 cups/1.5 L) Savoy or regular cabbage, cored and shredded

salt and freshly ground black pepper

2 leeks, green part only, washed and chopped

2 small zucchini, trimmed and finely chopped

1 cup (250 mL) fresh green beans, cut into ¾-inch (2-cm) pieces

In a large saucepan, combine the drained beans with 6 cups (1.5 L) cold water. Bring to a boil; reduce the heat to a simmer and cook for about an hour or until the beans are tender. Meanwhile, in a large frying pan, heat the olive oil over medium heat. Add the garlic, celery, onion and carrot and cook for 10 minutes or until the vegetables are softened.

When the beans are tender, stir the vegetable mixture into the beans (do not drain), along with the chicken broth, tomato paste, cabbage, salt and pepper. Bring to a boil; reduce the heat to simmer and cook for 10 minutes. Stir in the leeks and zucchini; cook for 15 minutes longer or until the vegetables are tender. Meanwhile, cook the green beans in a pan of boiling, salted water just until tender, about 3 minutes. Drain, plunge into cold water, and drain again. Add the beans to the soup a minute or so before serving.

For the pistou:

3–4 plump, fresh garlic cloves, peeled and finely chopped

1 tsp (5 mL) fine sea salt (or to taste)

2 cups (500 mL) loosely packed fresh basil leaves

½ cup (125 mL) extra virgin olive oil

½ cup (125 mL) freshly grated Parmesan cheese

Place the chopped garlic and salt in a mortar and, using a pestle, mash to form a paste. Add the basil leaves a few at a time, grinding and pounding with the pestle until a paste forms. Once all the leaves have been incorporated, start to add the olive oil a little at a time until a creamy consistency is reached. Taste for seasoning. Scrape the mixture into a small bowl and gently stir in the Parmesan until well incorporated.

Ladle the soup into warmed soup bowls. Place a good spoonful of the pistou into the centre of each serving and stir slightly. Serve with additional grated Parmesan cheese, if you wish, and good crusty bread and butter.

Bountiful Harvest Roasted Garlic & Potato Soup

Woodlawn Inn, Cobourg
Recommended: Inniskillin Wines Chardonnay Reserve
Makes 4–6 servings

This soup is the perfect choice for a rainy autumn day or a blustery winter evening. We have added our own touch with the cheese toasts. Don't worry about the amount of garlic; once it is baked, it becomes quite mellow.

For the soup:

2 heads garlic, intact
7 cups (1.75 L) chicken stock
4 large boiling potatoes, peeled and
    diced

1 cup (250 mL) Chardonnay
salt and freshly ground white pepper
    to taste

Preheat the oven to 375°F (190°C). Place the garlic heads in a little roasting pan and bake them for about 30 minutes, until soft. Bring the stock to a boil in a large saucepan, reduce the heat, add the potatoes and cook for 10 minutes. When the garlic is cool enough to handle, squeeze the cloves into the soup. Add the Chardonnay and season with salt and pepper. Simmer the soup for about 15 minutes.

For the cheese toasts:

½ cup (125 mL) extra virgin olive oil
1 baguette, cut diagonally into 1-inch
    (2.5-cm) slices
1 ½ cups (375 mL) ricotta cheese

1 cup (250 mL) grated Parmigiano-
    Reggiano cheese
¼ cup (50 mL) chopped flat-leaf
    parsley

Increase the oven temperature to 400°F (200°C). In a large frying pan, heat the olive oil on medium-high heat. In batches, toast the bread slices in the oil for about 1 minute per side, or until golden brown. Drain them on paper towelling. Divide the ricotta among the toasts, spreading it over the surface. Place the toasts on a baking sheet and sprinkle with some of the Parmigiano-Reggiano. Bake for 5 minutes, or until the cheese is golden. Sprinkle the toasts with parsley.

Ladle the soup into bowls and place one cheese toast in the centre of each. Serve the remaining toasts and cheese at the table.

Inniskillin

Inniskillin has become Canada's premier estate winery, with its motto "not so much bound by tradition as inspired by it" ringing true since its establishment in 1975.

The name Inniskillin—synonymous with quality Canadian icewine—is derived from the famous Irish regiment, the Inniskillin Fusilliers. One of their members, granted Crown land after the War of 1812, named his property the Inniskillin Farm.

Inniskillin has always produced wines with a distinctive Canadian character and has continued to grow and flourish, welcoming visitors from all over Ontario, Canada and the world to its winery.

Besides their Vidal Icewine (the most decorated Canadian wine) and Riesling Icewine, their offerings include single vineyard Chardonnays, Pinot Noir, Cabernet Sauvignon, Gamay Noir, Late Harvest Riesling and much more.

Organic Coconut Sweet Potato Soup

Grail Springs Health & Wellness Spa, Bancroft
Recommended: Inniskillin Wines Auxerrois
Makes 8 servings

Every Thursday, Chef Alexi Bracey conducts a Healthy Cooking Class at this inn that has a strong focus on balanced living. This simple-to-prepare yet exotically flavoured soup has only three ingredients plus a garnish. The success of the recipe depends on an excellent vegetable stock.

6 cups (1.5 L) organic vegetable stock
2 lb (1 kg) organic sweet potatoes, peeled and cut into pieces

3 cups (750 mL) organic coconut milk
8 fresh basil leaves, shredded

In a large soup pot over high heat, bring the vegetable stock to a boil. Add the sweet potatoes and cook until tender, about 15–20 minutes. Transfer ½ of the soup to a blender or food processor along with the coconut milk and purée until smooth. Return the purée to the other ½ of the soup in the pot. Reheat gently, stirring to combine well. Ladle into soup bowls and garnish with the shredded basil.

Wild Rice & Black Bean Soup

Sir Sam's Inn & WaterSpa, Haliburton
Recommended: Pelee Island Winery Cabernet Franc
Makes 8–10 servings

James Orr, innkeeper at Sir Sam's, says, "This hearty soup is a favourite with our guests. Served with fresh crusty bread, it's a meal in itself."

¼ cup (50 mL) butter
2 large leeks, trimmed, rinsed and
    chopped (white part only)
½ lb (250 g) ham, diced
⅓ cup (75 mL) all-purpose flour
12 cups (3 L) chicken stock

1 ½ cups (375 mL) wild rice
¾ cup (175 mL) dry sherry
14-oz (398-g) can black beans, drained
3 cups (750 mL) whipping cream
salt and freshly ground black pepper
    to taste

Melt the butter in a large soup pot over medium-high heat. Add the leeks and ham together and sauté for about 2–3 minutes. Stir in the flour and cook for another 2 minutes. Add the chicken stock to this mixture, whisking as you do to avoid lumps. Bring it to a gentle simmer. Add the rice and simmer until the rice is tender, about 45 minutes.

Transfer ½ of the mixture to a blender or food processor and purée. Return to the soup pot and add sherry, black beans and cream. Season with salt and pepper and simmer gently for about 20 minutes before serving.

Muskoka Premium Dark Ale & Cheddar Soup

Gananoque Inn, Gananoque
Recommended: Muskoka Premium Dark Ale or Henry of Pelham Family Estate Baco Noir
Makes 4–6 servings

The qualities of a well-made dark ale immeasurably enhance the sharp notes of great Canadian cheddar cheese in this traditional soup from the Gananoque Inn. Just the thing to precede a seared steak and lively green salad.

¼ cup (50 mL) butter
1 medium onion, chopped
⅓ cup (75 mL) all-purpose flour
4 cups (1 L) milk
1 bottle (341 mL) Muskoka Premium
  Dark Ale

2 cups (500 mL) shredded aged
  white cheddar
1 tsp (5 mL) salt
½ tsp (2 mL) white pepper

In a large saucepan, melt the butter over medium-high heat. Add the onion and sauté for 2–3 minutes or until it becomes translucent. Stir in the flour, coating the onions evenly, and cook for another minute or so. Add the milk gradually, using a whisk to prevent lumps. Now add the dark ale, stirring to blend all the liquids. Reduce the heat to medium-low and simmer the mixture, stirring occasionally. If it begins to stick on the bottom of the saucepan, lower the heat further. Add the cheese, a portion at a time, stirring well after each addition to help melt the cheese. Once all the cheese has been incorporated, transfer the mixture to a blender or food processor and process until smooth. Season with the salt and pepper and serve hot.

Four Onion Soup au Gratin

The Vintage Goose Inn & Spa, Kingsville
Recommended: Colio Estate Wines Gamay Noir
Makes 4 servings

This spin on the classic bistro favourite is intensified by including four members of the onion family as its base. You'll need 4 ovenproof bowls.

4 large Vidalia (or white) onions, very thinly sliced

2 large red onions, very thinly sliced

4 green onions, trimmed and finely chopped

2 leeks, trimmed, rinsed and very thinly sliced

¼ cup (50 mL) butter

1 Tbsp (15 mL) all-purpose flour

4 cups (1 L) beef broth

4 rounds bread, cut to fit the tops of the ovenproof soup bowls

½ tsp (2 mL) grated nutmeg

¼ cup (50 mL) cognac

salt and freshly ground black pepper to taste

½ lb (250 g) Emmentaler cheese, grated

In a large pot over medium-low heat, sauté all the onions and the leeks in the butter until golden. Mix in the flour and stir for 2–3 minutes to cook the flour. Add the broth, bring to a boil, then lower the heat and simmer for 1 hour.

Preheat the oven to 300°F (150°C). As the soup simmers, bake the bread rounds until toasted and dry, about 20 minutes. Remove from the oven and set aside. Turn the oven up to 450°F (230°C).

Add the nutmeg to the soup and simmer for 5 minutes. Add the cognac and remove from the heat.

Place salt and pepper and 2 Tbsp (25 mL) of the grated cheese in each of 4 ovenproof soup bowls. Divide the soup among them. Top each with a bread round. Divide the remaining cheese among the bowls and bake for 5 minutes or until the cheese melts. Turn on the broiler and crisp up the cheese. Serve immediately.

Goat Cheese Vinaigrette

Gananoque Inn, Gananoque
Makes ½ cup (125 mL)

A popular salad at the Gananoque Inn is one based on frisée and sun-dried tomatoes with this goat's milk cheese dressing. If you cannot easily obtain frisée, use romaine or radicchio or a combination of the two.

3 Tbsp (45 mL) goat's milk cheese
1 Tbsp (15 mL) water
3 Tbsp (45 mL) extra virgin olive oil

salt and freshly ground black pepper
to taste

In a small mixing bowl, cream the cheese together with the water and the olive oil until the desired consistency is reached. Season with salt and pepper. Store in a covered container and refrigerate.

Pomodori e Salame

The Waring House Inn, Picton
Recommended: Inniskillin Wines Pinot Gris
Makes 6–8 servings

This interesting summer salad at the peak of tomato season is a great choice when you're taking part in a potluck patio party.

4 oz (125 g) thinly sliced Genoa salami
(about 24 slices)
⅓ cup (75 mL) extra virgin olive oil
2 Tbsp (25 mL) fresh lemon juice
1 tsp (5 mL) finely chopped lemon zest
salt and freshly ground black pepper
to taste

1 garlic clove, minced
2 Tbsp (25 mL) chopped fresh basil
2 Tbsp (25 mL) chopped fresh flat-leaf
parsley
3 large ripe tomatoes

Place the salami slices in a shallow dish. Combine the oil, lemon juice, zest, salt, pepper, garlic, basil and 1 Tbsp (15 mL) of the parsley, and whisk to blend. Pour ½ of this mixture over the salami, lifting the slices up to allow the mixture to thoroughly coat them.

Cover with plastic wrap and leave at room temperature for about an hour, turning the slices once. Slice the tomatoes in ¼-inch (5-cm) slices. On a rectangular serving dish, arrange alternating slices of dressed salami and tomato. Pour the remaining dressing over all and garnish with the remaining chopped parsley.

Asparagus Soup

Inn at Manitou, McKellar
Cave Spring Cellars Sauvignon Blanc
Makes 6–8 servings

While most asparagus soup recipes rely on heavy cream to make them lustrous and rich, this lighter, no-cream, spa version is full of the unsullied flavours of fresh asparagus. Having said that, however, a little sour cream thinned with milk and drizzled over the surface, along with a length of chive, would make a pretty garnish.

2 lb (1 kg) fresh asparagus	handful of spinach leaves, chopped
2 Tbsp (25 mL) butter	6 cups (1.5 L) vegetable or chicken
2 shallots, finely chopped	stock
3 Tbsp (45 mL) chopped fresh chives	1 tsp (5 mL) salt
1 medium Yukon Gold potato (or other	¼ tsp (1 mL) white pepper
boiling potato), peeled and diced	

Snap off and discard the tough lower stems of the asparagus. With a vegetable peeler, scrape the lower part of the stalks. Cut off the tips and set aside. Cut the stalks into ½-inch (1-cm) pieces.

In a large saucepan over medium heat, melt the butter. Sauté the shallots for a minute or two until translucent; do not brown. Add the chives, potato, spinach, stock, salt and pepper and asparagus pieces (not the tips). Cover loosely and simmer for 30 minutes or until all the vegetables are quite tender.

Using a hand-held immersion blender, blender or food processor, purée the soup until smooth. (Make it ultra-smooth by then passing it through a sieve.) Briefly steam or microwave the asparagus tips until they are crisp-tender. Wipe the saucepan clean and return the soup to it along with the asparagus tips. Reheat gently, ladle into warmed soup bowls and serve immediately.

Prosciutto-Wrapped Roasted Figs on Arugula

The Inn at Christie's Mill, Port Severn
Strewn Winery Riesling Semi-Dry
Makes 8 servings

We love the combination of sweet anad savoury flavours in this Italian-inspired first course: the sweetness of the figs, the saltiness of the prosciutto, the pungent cheese and the slight bitterness afforded by the arugula.

For the vinaigrette:

½ shallot, minced

½ cup (125 mL) red wine vinegar

2 tsp (10 mL) honey

salt and freshly ground black pepper to taste

1 cup (250 mL) extra virgin olive oil

Put all the ingredients in a jar with a lid. Give it a good shake to blend the ingredients. Set to one side.

For the salad:

8 large ripe Black Mission figs

2 Tbsp (25 mL) pure maple syrup

freshly ground black pepper to taste

8 slices prosciutto

2 bunches arugula, washed, dried and trimmed

½ lb (250 g) Grana Padano cheese, shaved into thin slices

Preheat the oven to 425°F (220°C). Slice the stems off the figs and cut each fig ¾ of the way through the centre lengthwise. Drizzle a little maple syrup into the centre of each fig, then season with a little pepper. Close the figs and wrap each with a slice of prosciutto, securing with a toothpick if necessary. Place the wrapped figs on a tray and bake for 6–8 minutes, until the prosciutto is slightly crisp. As they are roasting, toss the arugula into a large mixing bowl and dress with the vinaigrette.

To serve, use tongs to mound a portion of dressed arugula on each of 8 plates. Top with a roasted fig and arrange the shaved cheese around it.

Baked Forelle Pear & Endive Salad

The Millcroft Inn & Spa, Alton
Recommended: Jackson-Triggs Proprietor's Reserve Riesling
Makes 1 serving

While this recipe makes just one serving, it can be doubled or tripled quite easily. As the sweet, small, colourful Forelle pears are usually just available from October to late winter, this is a lovely first course for that time of year. Make the blue cheese dressing first, then the filling, then roast, cool and fill the pear. It may seem a lot of fuss for an appetizer but the results are absolutely worth it, and almost everything can be done ahead of time.

For the dressing:

1 cup (250 mL) apple cider	1 whole bay leaf
2 whole star anise	2 cups (500 mL) whipping cream
2 whole cloves	2 Tbsp (25 mL) blue cheese

Heat the apple cider, star anise, cloves and bay leaf together in a saucepan placed over medium-high heat. Allow the mixture to come to a boil, reduce the heat and simmer until reduced to ¼ cup (50 mL). Add the cream and reduce again by ½. Add the blue cheese and stir to melt. Let the mixture cool. (When ready to use, if the dressing is too thick, thin with a little warm water.)

For the filling:

1 ½ tsp (7 mL) blue cheese, crumbled	1 ½ tsp (7 mL) dried cranberries, chopped
1 Tbsp (15 mL) toasted, chopped walnuts (reserve a little for garnish)	

Place all ingredients in a small mixing bowl and blend together well. Set to one side.

For the pear:

1 tsp (5 mL) butter, cubed

1 Forelle pear

½ tsp (2 mL) honey

Preheat the oven to 350°F (180°C). Place the butter cube on the pear stem, drizzle with honey and roast in the oven until cooked through, about 20 minutes. Remove from the oven and let cool. When cool, cut off the top and use a melon baller to scoop out the inside. Stuff with the cheese filling and chill.

To serve:

½ endive, separated

8 leaves mâche (also known as corn
     salad or lamb's lettuce)

¼ head frisée

Preheat the oven to 425°F (220°C). Warm the filled pear in the oven for approximately 5 minutes. Arrange the endive, mâche and frisée on a serving plate. Set the warmed pear in the centre. Drizzle the pear and greens with the dressing and garnish with the reserved walnuts. Serve immediately.

Spinach & Arugula Salad
with Warm Bacon & Shallot Vinaigrette

The Charles Inn, Niagara-on-the-Lake
Recommended: Pelee Island Winery Sauvignon Blanc
Makes 4 servings

The idea of a spinach and bacon salad may seem a tad old hat but when a thing is done well, one never grows tired of it. This version gives it some new twists. Use young spinach and arugula for the best results.

¼ lb (125 g) double-smoked bacon, finely diced

1 large shallot, finely chopped

1 tsp (5 mL) chopped fresh thyme leaves

1 Tbsp (15 mL) apple juice

3 Tbsp (45 mL) sherry vinegar

1 tsp (5 mL) Dijon mustard

2 Tbsp (25 mL) vegetable oil

2 Tbsp (25 mL) walnut oil

½ lb (250 g) baby spinach leaves

½ lb (250 g) baby arugula leaves

2 Tbsp (25 mL) toasted chopped walnuts

salt and freshly ground black pepper to taste

In a frying pan over medium heat, sauté the bacon until it is beginning to crisp, about 5 minutes. Add the shallot and thyme and continue to cook over low heat until the shallot begins to caramelize, about another 5 minutes. In a small mixing bowl, combine the apple juice, vinegar and mustard and slowly whisk in the two oils. Add the bacon and shallot mixture to the bowl and stir to combine well. Keep the mixture warm. Toss the greens into a mixing bowl, add the chopped nuts, dress with the warm vinaigrette and season with salt and pepper. Serve immediately on individual serving plates.

Apple, Cheese & Walnut Salad

Rosemount Inn, Kingston
Recommended: Henry of Pelham Family Estate Off-dry Riesling
Makes 6 servings

Reminiscent of the classic Waldorf salad—apples, celery, mayonnaise and, later, walnuts—this bright-tasting salad has great crunch appeal; adding a bit of chopped celery would make it even more so. Great as a partner to grilled chicken or pork.

3 Tbsp (45 mL) olive oil
2 Tbsp (25 mL) balsamic vinegar
2 tsp (10 mL) Dijon mustard
1 garlic clove, minced
freshly ground black pepper to taste
8 cups (2 L) torn, mixed salad greens

2 medium Fuji apples, halved, cored and sliced ⅛-inch (.3-cm) thick
⅓ cup (75 mL) crumbled blue cheese
¼ cup (50 mL) coarsely chopped toasted walnuts

In a small mixing bowl, whisk together the olive oil, vinegar, mustard, garlic and pepper. In another mixing bowl, combine the greens and apple slices. Drizzle the vinaigrette over the greens and toss together well. Distribute the salad among 6 plates. Top each with a portion of blue cheese and toasted walnuts.

Mixed Greens with Gorgonzola & Maple-Infused Pears with Honey Peppercorn Vinaigrette

Sir Sam's Inn & WaterSpa, Haliburton
Recommended: Cave Spring Cellars Riesling Reserve
Makes 4 servings

Another variation on the theme of blue cheese, assorted greens and pears, this recipe is a favourite at Sir Sam's. This combination of salad greens, raddicchio, frisée and romaine may be varied as you wish. However, to balance overall flavours, be sure to combine slightly bitter greens with one or two mild-mannered varieties as the chef has done here. If you like, toast a few pine nuts or sliced almonds to use as a garnish.

For the vinaigrette:

1 ½ cups (375 mL) canola oil
¼ cup (50 mL) fresh lemon juice
¼ cup (50 mL) white wine vinegar
1 tsp (5 mL) salt
1 tsp (5 mL) granulated sugar

1 tsp (5 mL) paprika
2 tsp (10 mL) pink peppercorns, packed in brine (drain)
¼ cup (50 mL) liquid honey

Combine all the vinaigrette ingredients in a jar with a tight-fitting lid and shake thoroughly.

For the salad:

2 Tbsp (25 mL) olive oil
¼ cup (50 mL) pure maple syrup
2 Anjou pears, cored and sliced
1 head radicchio, shredded
1 head frisée, shredded

1 head romaine lettuce, coarsely chopped
½ lb (225 g) Gorgonzola cheese, cubed

In a medium-sized saucepan, warm the olive oil over medium-high heat. Blend in the maple syrup, then add the pear slices and stir to coat well with the mixture. Sauté the pears for 3 minutes until glazed. Set to one side.

Combine the salad greens in a large bowl and toss together. Drizzle a little of the vinaigrette over the greens, just enough to make the leaves glisten. Place the greens on individual salad plates. Arrange the cubed cheese and sliced pears on each salad and drizzle with additional vinaigrette. (You may not need all of the vinaigrette; store any leftovers in a covered container for up to 5 days and refrigerate.) Serve immediately.

Grilled Peach & Buffalo Mozzarella Salad with Tender Greens

Inn on the Twenty, Jordan
Cave Spring Cellars 2004 Pinot Gris
Makes 6 servings

There are 4 easy-to-assemble components to this summery salad: the greens themselves, pungent pesto, a zesty olive tapenade and peach salsa. Luscious ripe peaches add lots of flavour and colour to this distinctive first course. While the chef uses a variety of peaches with different coloured flesh for this recipe, any fresh peaches may be used. Great as a precursor to summer grills of chicken or pork—especially since you will require the grill to cook the peaches. Make the pesto, tapenade and salsa ahead of time but remove them from the refrigerator at least half an hour before serving.

For the pesto:

¼ cup (50 mL) basil leaves
¼ cup (50 mL) arugula leaves
¼ cup (50 mL) grated Parmesan
   cheese
1 garlic clove

1 Tbsp (15 mL) fresh thyme leaves
approximately ½ cup (125 mL) extra
   virgin olive oil
salt and freshly ground black pepper
   to taste

Combine the basil, arugula, cheese, garlic and thyme in the bowl of a food processor or blender and process using the on/off button. With the motor running, add the oil gradually until a smooth paste forms. Season with salt and pepper. Scrape into a small bowl and set aside.

For the olive tapenade:

1 shallot, quartered
½ cup (125 mL) pitted black olives,
   preferably oil-cured

1 tsp (5 mL) grated lemon zest
2 pieces sun-dried tomato
1 Tbsp (15 mL) extra virgin olive oil

The Breadalbane Inn

The Vintage Goose Inn & Spa

The Carmichael Inn & Spa

Inn on the Twenty

Drinks in the garden at The Breadalbane Inn

The Inn at Christie's Mill

Pub at Kettle Creek Inn

The dining room at Trinity House Inn

Combine the shallot, olives, lemon zest and sun-dried tomato in the bowl of a food processor or blender and process using the on/off button. With the motor running, add the oil gradually until a smooth paste forms. Scrape into a small bowl and set aside.

For the peach salsa:

3 firm peaches, rubbed with a coarse towel to remove the fuzz, halved, pitted and finely diced

1 small shallot, finely diced

2 basil leaves, chopped

3 Tbsp (45 mL) liquid honey

2 Tbsp (25 mL) extra virgin olive oil

salt and freshly ground black pepper to taste

Combine all the ingredients in a small bowl, and toss to combine well. Set aside.

For the salad:

3 firm peaches, rubbed with a coarse towel to remove fuzz, halved and pitted

¼ cup (50 mL) extra virgin olive oil

salt and freshly ground black pepper to taste

6 cups (1.5 L) mixed greens

six ¼-inch thick (5-cm) slices buffalo mozzarella

Slice each peach half into two rounds (4 slices from each peach). Brush each slice on both sides with a little of the olive oil. Sprinkle with salt and pepper. Grill on each side just until grill marks appear, about 1 minute per side.

In a large mixing bowl, toss the greens with the remaining olive oil and a little salt and pepper. Distribute the greens among 6 salad plates. Arrange 2 peach slices and 2 mozzarella slices alternately on each serving and top with a spoonful each of salsa, pesto and tapenade.

Quinoa & Pepper Salad with Merlot Vinaigrette

Claramount Inn & Spa
Recommended: Henry of Pelham Family Estate Non-Oaked Chardonnay
Makes 4 servings

The vinaigrette for this high-protein grain and vegetable salad uses three different vinegars, one of which is Merlot-based. If you can't easily obtain Merlot vinegar, increase the quantity of red wine vinegar accordingly, or simply substitute Merlot. Use your taste buds to reach the right balance of acid to oil.

For the vinaigrette:

1 shallot, minced
1 tsp (5 mL) minced ginger
¼ cup (50 mL) chopped fresh herbs
   (basil, parsley, thyme)
¼ cup (50 mL) red wine vinegar

¼ cup (50 mL) rice wine vinegar
½ cup (125 mL) Merlot vinegar
1 ½ cups (375 mL) extra virgin olive oil
2 Tbsp (25 mL) pure maple syrup

Combine all the vinaigrette ingredients in a jar with a tight-fitting lid and shake thoroughly. Set to one side.

For the salad:

1 cup (250 mL) cooked quinoa (or other
   favourite cooked grain)
½ apple, cored and roughly chopped
¼ cup (50 mL) golden or dark raisins
   (or a combination of both)
1 small red onion, very thinly sliced

½ small red bell pepper, seeded and
   diced
½ small yellow bell pepper, seeded
   and diced
2 oz (50 g) blue cheese, crumbled

In a large mixing bowl, combine all the salad ingredients except the cheese. Toss together to blend. Add ⅓ cup (75 mL) of the vinaigrette and toss again. Arrange the salad on serving plates and top each with a little blue cheese. Drizzle with more vinaigrette and serve immediately. (You won't need all of the vinaigrette; store the remainder in a covered container and refrigerate for up to 5 days.)

Smoked Summer Tomato Soup

Sam Jakes Inn, Merrickville
Recommended: Jackson-Triggs Cabernet Franc-Cabernet Sauvignon Proprietor's Reserve
Makes 4–6 servings

This intriguing soup is from Thomas Riding, the Scottish-born chef who has been at Sam Jakes since 2002. You'll need a portable smoker for this recipe; the chef recommends red cedar sticks to create the fragrant smoke.

12 vine-ripened tomatoes, quartered
2 Tbsp (25 mL) olive oil
salt and freshly ground black pepper
　　to taste
2 large onions, thickly sliced

4 garlic cloves
1 bunch fresh basil
2 cups (500 mL) canned, chopped
　　plum tomatoes and their juice
12 leaves fresh basil, cut into strips

Prepare the smoker according to the manufacturer's directions. Toss the tomatoes with 1 Tbsp (15 mL) of the olive oil, salt and pepper. Add the onion and garlic and toss with the tomatoes. Place the vegetables on the rack of the smoker and hot-smoke for 20–30 minutes or until soft and well-smoked.

Transfer the vegetables to a soup pot, add the remaining olive oil and sauté the vegetables for a few minutes before adding the canned tomatoes and their juice. Cook for a further 30 minutes before puréeing with a hand-held immersion blender. Heat the soup through again and serve garnished with fresh basil.

Prince Edward County Rustic Grilled Cheese Sandwich

Merrill Inn, Picton
Recommended: Inniskillin Wines Cabernet Franc
Makes 4 servings

At the Merrill Inn, this signature luncheon dish—a modern tribute to a Canadian favourite—is served with seasoned potato chips, dressed baby greens and a spiced pear and tomato chutney (one of a number of Merrill Inn foodstuffs you can purchase there and in specialty food shops).

¼ cup (50 mL) unsalted butter, at room temperature
2 Tbsp (25 mL) pure maple syrup
8 slices good-quality multi-grain bread
1 lb (500 g) extra-aged cheddar cheese, sliced
4 slices Black Forest ham
2 McIntosh apples, sliced

In a small mixing bowl, cream together the butter and maple syrup. Set to one side.

Make 4 sandwiches using the bread, cheese, ham and apple slices. Spread each outside slice of bread with the butter and maple syrup spread. Preheat the oven to 250°F (120°C). Set a non-stick frying pan over medium-high heat. Brown each sandwich on both sides. Transfer the sandwiches to a tray and place in the oven to thoroughly melt the cheese, about 6 minutes. Cut on the diagonal and serve.

Steak & Portobello Mushroom Sandwich

The Westover Inn, St. Marys
Recommended: Pelee Island Winery Cabernet Sauvignon
Makes 4 servings

For the following simple preparation, the chef recommends using a bread with rosemary in its makeup. Waring House's recipe for Rosemary Focaccia on page 102 is perfect.

2 Tbsp (25 mL) Worcestershire sauce
2 Tbsp (25 mL) olive oil
salt and freshly ground black pepper
    to taste
1 lb (500 g) sirloin steak
1 Tbsp (15 mL) unsalted butter
1 Tbsp (15 mL) olive oil
2 large portobello mushrooms (remove
    black gills), sliced

1 rosemary focaccia, halved
    horizontally, and evenly cut into
    4 squares (8 pieces)
¼ cup (50 mL) unsalted butter
¼ cup (50 mL) coarse-grained Dijon
    mustard

In a shallow dish, whisk together the Worcestershire sauce and the 2 Tbsp (25 mL) olive oil. Lay the steak in the dish and turn it over once or twice to coat with the mixture. Season the steak well with salt and pepper. Cover with plastic wrap and let marinate for about an hour.

Preheat the grill to high. While it is heating, put the butter and the 1 Tbsp (15 mL) oil in a frying pan over medium-high heat. Add the mushrooms and sauté until softened and beginning to caramelize, about 15 minutes. Keep warm. Place the steak on the grill and cook for about 3–4 minutes per side or to desired doneness. Transfer the steak to a cutting board, cover with foil and let rest for 5 minutes.

Spread butter on each of the focaccia squares and grill, buttered side down, for less than a minute, just until grill marks begin to show. Remove from the grill and spread mustard on ½ of each square.

Thinly slice the steak and distribute the slices onto each of the four squares of bread. Add a few portobello slices and the top of the bread. Serve immediately.

Harbour House Potted Cheese

Harbour House Hotel, Niagara-on-the-Lake
Recommended: Strewn Winery Cabernet Franc or a dark ale
Makes 8 servings

This is an addictive little spread that's absolutely delicious when teamed with crusty bread, crackers, crudités and a good dark ale. Packed into attractive crocks or ramekins, this makes a great gift at holiday time.

1 lb (500 g) assorted cheeses, cut into small pieces

1 (341 mL) bottle dark ale

.2 Tbsp (25 mL) horseradish (or more to taste)

2 Tbsp (25 mL) tomato chili sauce (or more to taste)

1 Tbsp (15 mL) Dijon mustard

½ tsp (2 mL) hot chili pepper flakes

½ tsp (2 mL) garlic powder

Place the cheese in a food processor and process dry for 2–3 minutes, just to break up the larger bits. Add a small amount of ale, process briefly and check the consistency. If needed, add more ale to achieve the desired consistency, blending for a minute or two. With the motor running, add the remaining ingredients and continue to blend. (The longer you blend, the smoother the end result will be.) Transfer the mixture to a container with a lid and keep refrigerated until ready to serve.

Brandied Herb Pâté

The Little Inn of Bayfield, Bayfield
Recommended: Henry of Pelham Family Estate Gamay
Makes 8 servings

Serve this with thinly sliced baguette or good white bakery bread, toasted and crusts trimmed. A little dish of gherkins is nice, too.

1 Tbsp (15 mL) butter
1 onion, chopped
2 garlic cloves, minced
½ tsp (2 mL) chopped fresh thyme
1 lb (500 g) chicken livers, cleaned of membranes and halved
¼ cup (50 mL) cream cheese
¼ cup (50 mL) brandy or port

2 Tbsp (25 mL) finely chopped fresh parsley
½ tsp (2 mL) dried mustard
¼ tsp (1 mL) ground cloves
¼ tsp (1 mL) allspice
¼ tsp (1 mL) salt
¼ tsp (1 mL) freshly ground black pepper

In a frying pan, melt the butter over medium heat; cook the onion, garlic and thyme, stirring often, for 3 minutes or until softened. Add the chicken livers and cook, stirring often, for 8 minutes or until the livers have just a touch of pink inside. Remove from the heat and let stand for 5 minutes.

In a food processor, purée the liver mixture with the remaining ingredients until smooth. Transfer to a serving bowl (or smaller individual ramekins). Place plastic wrap directly on the surface and refrigerate for at least 4 hours or until quite firm.

Classic Crab Cakes

Merrill Inn, Picton
Recommended: Inniskillin Wines Unoaked Chardonnay
Makes 4–6 servings

The chef at Merrill Inn likes to serve this perennial favourite over a bed of dressed greens. If you choose to, you could make these a little smaller and serve them as cocktail fare. Don't forget the tartar sauce and fresh lemon wedges.

1 large egg, lightly beaten
2 Tbsp (25 mL) mayonnaise
1 tsp (5 mL) Dijon mustard
1 tsp (5 mL) Worcestershire sauce
1 Tbsp (15 mL) Old Bay Seasoning
½ red onion, diced
1 celery stalk, diced
½ red bell pepper, diced
1 Tbsp (15 mL) finely chopped chives

½ cup (125 mL) fresh breadcrumbs
1 lb (500 g) cooked crabmeat (fresh or frozen), picked over to remove any shell or cartilage and pulled apart into chunks
salt and freshly ground black pepper to taste
2 Tbsp (25 mL) unsalted butter
2 Tbsp (25 mL) vegetable oil

In a large bowl, combine the egg, mayonnaise, mustard, Worcestershire sauce, Old Bay Seasoning, onion, celery, red pepper and chives. Mix well, then add the breadcrumbs, crabmeat, salt and pepper. Using a fork, blend the ingredients together well. Divide the mixture into 8 equal portions (or smaller if you wish). Shape each one into a patty about 2 inches (5 cm) in diameter and about ¾ inch (2 cm) thick.

In a large frying pan, warm ½ the butter and oil over medium-high heat. Fry ½ of the crab cakes for about 4 minutes on each side until golden brown on both sides, turning once with a spatula. Repeat with the remaining butter, oil and crab cakes. Serve immediately.

Red Onion & Apple Marmalade

Benmiller Inn & Spa
Makes about 1 ½ cups (375 mL)

A delightful condiment that has been a constant at the Benmiller Inn & Spa where it's used very effectively with the rich house pâté. It is also terrific in sandwiches, with grilled sausage, pork or ham, alongside sharp cheddar or in cold meat sandwiches.

2 Tbsp (25 mL) butter	½ cup (125 mL) red wine
2 Tbsp (25 mL) extra virgin olive oil	⅓ cup (75 mL) red wine vinegar
8 cups (2 L) sliced red onions	½ cup (125 mL) apple cider
3 Tbsp (45 mL) granulated sugar	2 Tbsp (25 mL) honey
1 ½ tsp (7 mL) salt	4 cups (1 L) cored, peeled and
½ tsp (2 mL) ground cloves	sliced McIntosh apples (about 3
½ tsp (2 mL) ground cinnamon	medium-sized apples)

In a large saucepan, melt the butter in the oil over low heat. Add the onions and stir to coat with the mixture. Cover loosely and cook for 10 minutes, stirring occasionally. Add the sugar, salt, cloves, cinnamon, wine, vinegar, cider and honey. Stir well and continue cooking uncovered until the onions are quite soft, 20 minutes or so. Add the apples and cook for a further 15 minutes, until they begin to soften and the whole mixture becomes thick and jam-like. Remove from the heat and allow to cool. Pack into hot, sterilized glass jars and store in the refrigerator for up to a month.

Ontario Ham Hock & Parsley Terrine

The Elora Mill Inn
Recommended: Cave Spring Cellars Dry Rosé
Makes 4–6 servings

This is very good with old-fashioned mustard pickle or any chutney. Prepare to make this a day in advance.

2 fresh ham hocks, about 4 lb (2 kg)
  in total
¼ cup (50 mL) white wine vinegar
1 onion, chopped
1 carrot, chopped
1 celery stalk, chopped
1 small leek, rinsed and chopped
6 whole cloves
4 fresh thyme sprigs
6 garlic cloves
10 whole black peppercorns
1 large bunch flat-leaf parsley finely
  chopped
salt and freshly ground black pepper
  to taste

Place the ham hocks in a Dutch oven or similar heavy pot, cover with cold water and bring to a boil over high heat. When it has boiled, drain and discard the water. Add enough cold water to cover the ham hocks. Add the vinegar, chopped vegetables, cloves, thyme, garlic and peppercorns. Return to a boil over high heat, then reduce the heat and simmer for 3–4 hours, until the ham hocks are tender. Make sure the ham hocks remain submerged, adding a little additional water if necessary.

Using tongs, transfer the hocks to a plate or cutting board to cool. Strain the cooking liquid into a bowl. You will need ⅔ cup (150 mL) of the liquid (freeze the rest for soup).

When the hocks are cool, line a pâté baking dish (or small loaf pan) with plastic wrap, allowing it to overhang slightly. Using a small paring knife, pull off and discard the ham hock skin. Remove the meat from the bone, discarding all the fat as you work. Using your fingers, tear the meat into rough chunks and cover the bottom of the baking dish with it until you have a substantial layer. Scatter the surface generously with chopped parsley and season with salt and pepper. Repeat the layers until all the ham and parsley are used, ending with the ham. Pour the reserved cooking liquid over top. Cover with more plastic wrap and place a weight on top (a large can will do). Refrigerate overnight, or until firm.

Cave Spring Cellars

Situated on the Beamsville Bench, tucked into the town of Jordan, the Cave Spring Estate was first planted in 1978, making it one of Niagara's most mature vinifera vineyards. Company founder Leonard Pennachetti and winemaker Angelo Pavan have always held fast to the philosophy that great wines are grown, not made, a truism that visitors happily attest to whether they visit the winery shop for tastings, or enjoy lunch or dinner at the Inn on the Twenty, the first critically acclaimed restaurant in wine country. In 1993, they opened The Vintner's Inn, adjacent to the winery, an artfully designed operation that's the work of Helen Young, Leonard's wife. Cave Spring Cellars features a variety of wines, including Riesling, Sauvignon Blanc, Chardonnay, Cabernet Merlot and Riesling icewine.

Portobello Mushrooms & Burgundy Escargots with Herbes de Provence

Domain of Killien
Recommended: Inniskillin Pinot Noir Reserve
Makes 4 servings

You can't get much more French than this delightful first-course offering. While the escargots in question are canned, they are of good quality and lend an authentic French accent to this simple appetizer that never fails to impress. Chef Daniel Ricart recommends serving these with a pesto or homemade tomato sauce, although they are very good just as they are. Make sure to offer good crusty bread and butter alongside.

4 large portobello mushrooms	salt and freshly ground black pepper
5 Tbsp (75 mL) extra virgin olive oil	to taste
3 Tbsp (45 mL) herbes de Provence	½ cup (125 mL) vegetable stock
200-g can imported escargots	(optional)
2 shallots, finely chopped	4 cups (1 L) mesclun greens
2 Tbsp (25 mL) pastis (or Pernod)	¼ cup (50 mL) chopped fresh parsley

Preheat the oven to 350°F (180°C). Wipe the portobellos clean with a damp cloth and remove the stems (reserve for another use, such as vegetable stock). Remove the black gills and discard. Line a tray with parchment paper and lay the mushrooms, cavity side down, on the tray. Brush the tops of the mushrooms with 2 Tbsp (25 mL) of the olive oil and sprinkle 2 Tbsp (25 mL) of the herbes de Provence over the mushrooms, rubbing it through your fingers to crumble. Bake the mushrooms in the oven for about 8 minutes.

Drain the escargots and rinse well. Warm another 2 Tbsp (25 mL) of the olive oil in a frying pan over medium-high heat and pan-fry the escargots for 2 minutes, stirring now and then. Add the shallots to the pan. Rub the remaining herbes de Provence through your fingers onto the escargots in the pan and cook for a further 2 minutes. Add the pastis (or Pernod) and carefully ignite the pan's juices. Let the flames die down, then season with salt and pepper. If you are using the vegetable stock, add it now. Allow everything to come to a gentle boil, then immediately reduce the heat to low and let it simmer until the liquid has reduced, about 4 minutes.

To serve, place the mesclun greens in a large bowl and toss together with the remaining olive oil and a bit of salt and pepper. Evenly distribute the greens among 4 serving plates. Place the mushroom caps, cavity side up, atop the greens. Fill each with some of the escargot and their pan juices. Sprinkle each with a little parsley and serve immediately.

Note: Unless you want to go to the extreme step of gathering, purging and cooking your own snails, you'll want to purchase prepared snails. These are widely available in cans imported from France. A 200-g can will contain either 4 dozen small, 3 dozen medium or 2 dozen large snails. Choose the small snails for this recipe. Since canned snails are cooked in a savoury broth and some of that liquid is used in the canning process, make sure to drain the snails and rinse with running water before using.

Rosemary Focaccia

The Waring House Inn, Picton
Recommended: Jackson-Triggs Proprietor's Reserve Sauvignon Blanc
Makes 1 focaccia

The Cookery School at the Waring House is a year-round facility offering hands-on recreational cooking classes in a spacious environment just next to the inn. Classes may be paired with wine tours or include sommelier-led wine tastings. This recipe for a potato-based focaccia is a class favourite. In the interests of efficiency, make extra mashed potato for dinner one evening before you plan on making this recipe as the leftovers will work well here.

For the caramelized onions:

1 large onion	1 Tbsp (15 mL) granulated sugar
2 Tbsp (25 mL) butter	

Thinly slice the onion and sauté in the butter until translucent, about 10 minutes. Add the sugar and continue to sauté over medium heat until the onions are golden brown and caramelized.

For the focaccia:

2 Tbsp (25 mL) fresh rosemary leaves	1 Tbsp (15 mL) olive oil
1 cup (250 mL) boiling water	1 cup (250 mL) mashed potato
1 Tbsp (15 mL) granulated sugar	2 ½ cups (625 mL) all-purpose flour
1 Tbsp (15 mL) active dry yeast	2 tsp (10 mL) olive oil
1 tsp (5 mL) salt	coarse salt to taste

Place 1 Tbsp (15 mL) of the rosemary in a medium-sized bowl and pour the boiling water over the leaves. Let the mixture cool to lukewarm (don't let the water cool completely).

Strain the water, discarding the rosemary. Add the sugar to the water and stir to dissolve. Sprinkle the yeast over the water and let stand for 10 minutes until foamy. Stir the salt and the 1 Tbsp (15 mL) olive oil into the yeast mixture. Stir in the mashed potato and add the flour gradually, stirring well after each addition. Once a dough forms, turn it out onto a lightly floured surface. Knead until it is smooth and elastic, about 10 minutes. Clean the bread bowl and oil lightly. Transfer the dough to the bowl and cover with plastic wrap. Let rise in a warm place for 45 minutes.

Punch the dough down and knead 1 minute more, adding a little flour if the dough seems sticky. Let rest for 5 minutes.

Turn the dough out onto a lightly floured surface. Spread the dough onto a well-greased baking sheet with sides. Brush with the 2 tsp (10 mL) olive oil and sprinkle with coarse salt. Scatter the caramelized onions over top. Roughly chop the remaining 1 Tbsp (15 mL) of rosemary and scatter over the surface. Cover loosely with plastic wrap and let rise in a warm place for 30 minutes.

A few minutes before the time is up, preheat the oven to 400°F (200°C). Remove the plastic and bake the focaccia for 10 minutes, then reduce the heat to 375°F (190°C). Bake for another 12 minutes, or until the bread is puffed and golden brown and the sides are shrinking away from the sides of the baking sheet. The bread should sound hollow when tapped on the bottom.

Let the bread cool on the baking sheet for 10 minutes, then transfer to a rack to cool. Serve warm with extra virgin olive oil alongside for dipping.

Thai Salad Rolls

The Millcroft Inn & Spa, Alton
Recommended: Pelee Island Winery Gewürtztraminer
Makes 4 servings

Nothing could be easier to assemble than these fresh-tasting vegetarian spring rolls—perfect fare for enjoying on a patio on a hot summer day. The Millcroft's version includes a non-traditional ingredient in the form of jicama (a Mexican root vegetable with a mild, nutty flavour), but almost any crunchy, colourful, thinly sliced vegetables may be used, as we do in this variation. Most large supermarkets carry the rice paper wraps. (Or look for them in Asian food shops.) The secret to ease of preparation is to have all the ingredients ready ahead of time, ready to be rolled into the wraps.

For the dipping sauce:

½ cup (125 mL) hoisin sauce
2 Tbsp (25 mL) sesame oil
3 Tbsp (45 mL) light soy sauce
¾ tsp (4 mL) hot chili sauce

juice of 1 lime
2 garlic cloves, minced
1 Tbsp (15 mL) minced fresh ginger

Combine all the ingredients in a small mixing bowl and whisk together. Set aside while you prepare the rolls.

For the rolls:

8 large rice paper wraps
1 ½ cups (375 mL) shredded romaine
    lettuce
½ cup (125 mL) celery, cut into
    matchstick
½ cup (125 mL) seedless cucumber,
    cut into matchstick strips

½ cup (125 mL) mango, cut into
    matchstick strips
½ cup (125 mL) red bell pepper,
    cut into matchstick strips
1 cup (250 mL) bean sprouts
2 green onions, trimmed, cut into
    thirds, then shredded lengthwise

(ingredients continue next page)

4 fresh mint leaves
4 fresh basil leaves

8 coriander sprigs

Fill a wide bowl with tepid water. Dip a rice paper wrap in the water, leaving it immersed just long enough to soften and turn white, about 40 seconds. Carefully lift it out and spread it on a clean tea towel. Repeat with the remaining rice paper wraps.

Divide the ingredients evenly among the rice paper wraps, placing the vegetables and fruit on top of each other in the centre of each one. Carefully turn in 1 edge of a wrap, then the 2 sides and finally roll it into a cylinder; be careful not to tear the rice paper. Repeat with the remaining wraps. When all the rolls have been assembled, use a sharp chef's knife to carefully slice each roll diagonally into bite-sized pieces (larger if you prefer) and arrange on a serving platter. Pour the sauce into 1 or 2 small ramekins and serve alongside for dipping.

Riverbend Inn Cornbread

Riverbend Inn & Vineyard, Niagara-on-the-Lake
Makes 1 large loaf (serves 8–10 people)

A delightful, easy-to-make bread that is perfect with a bowl of hearty soup or chili. This freezes well.

2 cups (475 mL) cornmeal
4 cups (1 L) all-purpose flour
2 tsp (10 mL) baking powder
1 tsp (5 mL) baking soda
2 tsp (10 mL) salt
2 eggs beaten
2 cups (475 mL) buttermilk

2 Tbsp (25 mL) vegetable oil
4–5 chopped chipotle peppers
 in adobe sauce (these are in
 canned form available in most
 supermarkets or food shops)
1 bunch chives, chopped

Blend all wet ingredients together then add the dry ingredients and mix. Transfer the mixture into a well-greased loaf pan and bake at 350°F (175°C) degrees for 45 minutes.

Black Bean & Wild Mushroom Bruschetta

Sir Sam's Inn & WaterSpa, Haliburton
Recommended: Henry of Pelham Family Estate Pinot Noir Unfiltered
Makes 4–6 servings

Savoury black beans and assorted mushrooms combine with tomatoes and sweet peppers to make an attractive appetizer. Vary the mushrooms as you wish, using cremini, oyster, shiitake, chanterelle and portobello, or whatever is readily available.

1 cup (250 mL) black beans, drained	4 cilantro sprigs, finely chopped
½ lb (250 g) assorted mushrooms, wiped clean and finely chopped	juice of 1 lime
8 plum tomatoes, diced	1 pinch each, ground cumin, salt and freshly ground black pepper
1 yellow bell pepper, seeded and diced	½ cup (125 mL) extra virgin olive oil
1 medium red onion, diced	1 baguette, thinly sliced
	½ cup (120 mL) grated Asiago cheese

In a medium-sized bowl, combine the black beans, mushrooms, tomatoes, bell pepper, onion, cilantro, lime juice, seasonings and olive oil. Mix to thoroughly combine, cover with plastic wrap and marinate for 2–3 hours to allow the flavours to develop.

Preheat the oven to 350°F (180°C). Place the baguette slices on a baking tray. Use a slotted spoon to divide the bean and vegetable mixture among the slices of bread. Top each one with cheese. Bake for 10 minutes or until heated through and the cheese is beginning to brown. Serve hot or warm.

Main Courses
Spring

Whether your visit to one of Ontario's finest inns is timed for early spring, when snow and wintry conditions may still be lingering, or for a time when spring is in full beautiful swing, nowhere is the start of the green season more keenly felt.

Chefs at the inns look forward to the spring season with great enthusiasm, devising menus that feature the best that area growers have to offer. You'll find lighter entrées of fish and shellfish, lamb, chicken and veal with green accents of fresh asparagus, young leeks, fiddleheads and those other bright-tasting harbingers of spring, morels and early rhubarb.

Chapter Three

MAIN COURSES—SPRING

Ricotta Gnocchi with Creamed Leeks

The Briars Resort & Spa, Jackson's Point
Recommended: Colio Estate Wines CEV Chardonnay
Makes 6 servings

Gnocchi based on ricotta cheese rather than potato are unfailingly light and airy. Just make sure not to add too much flour or overwork the dough. Chef Trevor Ledlie of The Briars accents this perfect-for-spring dish with strips of prosciutto and fresh steamed spinach.

For the creamed leeks:

1 Tbsp (15 mL) butter	2 leeks, trimmed, rinsed well and
1 Tbsp (15 mL) olive oil	thinly sliced
1 shallot, diced	1 cup (250 mL) white wine
1 garlic clove, minced	1 cup (250 mL) whipping cream

In a medium saucepan, melt the butter with the olive oil over medium-high heat. Sauté the shallot and garlic until golden brown. Add the leeks and white wine and reduce to low heat; cook for 20 minutes. Add the cream and cook for a further 20 minutes. Set aside.

For the gnocchi:

1 lb (500 g) ricotta cheese	½ cup (125 mL) grated Parmigiano-
2 eggs	Reggiano cheese
2 egg yolks	1 ½ cups (375 mL) all-purpose flour
pinch salt	(approximate)

Place the ricotta in a sieve set over a bowl. Let stand for a few minutes if the ricotta is quite wet. Discard the liquids and wipe the bowl clean. In the same bowl, stir together the drained ricotta, eggs, egg yolks, salt and ½ the Parmigiano-Reggiano with a wooden spoon until well mixed. Stir in 1 cup (250 mL) flour, ¼ cup (50 mL) at a time. Stir in enough of the remaining flour to make a firm but soft dough.

Using a 1 Tbsp (15 mL) measuring spoon, portion out the dough and shape into small dumplings, more oval than round. Place on a large baking sheet lined with waxed paper, spacing them apart so they don't stick to each other.

Bring a large pot of lightly salted water to a boil. Cook the gnocchi in batches of a dozen at a time for 5 minutes or until they bob to the surface of the water. Remove with a slotted spoon to a warm serving dish.

Reheat the creamed leeks, if necessary. Pour over the warm gnocchi and serve immediately.

Fennel, Sweet Pea & Basil Risotto

Trinity House Inn, Gananoque
Makes 2 servings as a main course, 4 as an appetizer
Recommended: Strewn Winery Chardonnay-Pinot Blanc

A fresh-tasting risotto with flavours that would team well with grilled fish or any seafood.

6 cups (1.5 L) chicken stock
¼ cup (50 mL) fresh basil, finely
    chopped
6 Tbsp (90 mL) extra virgin olive oil
2 medium onions, coarsely chopped
1 medium fennel bulb, trimmed and
    coarsely chopped
½ cup (125 mL) dry white wine
1 cup (250 mL) Italian Arborio rice

1 ½ cups (375 mL) fresh sweet peas
½ cup (125 mL) grated Pecorino
    Romano cheese
2 Tbsp (25 mL) butter
¼ cup (50 mL) grated Parmigiano-
    Reggiano cheese
¼ cup (50 mL) finely chopped flat-leaf
    parsley

In a large saucepan, bring the chicken stock to simmer and add the basil.

In a large non-stick frying pan, heat 3 Tbsp (45 mL) of the olive oil over medium-low heat. Add the onion and fennel, cover and cook until the vegetables are soft, about 10 minutes. Remove to a separate bowl. In the same pan, combine the remaining 3 Tbsp (45 mL) olive oil and rice. Stir well to coat the rice with the oil. Return the onions and fennel to the pan. Add the white wine and simmer gently until the wine reduces by about ¾.

Add 1–2 ladles of the simmering stock to the rice, making sure to cover the rice and vegetables completely with the stock. Stir and simmer over low heat until the liquid is absorbed. Add the same amount of stock again, just until the vegetables and rice are covered. Repeat this process, stirring frequently, until the rice becomes creamy in texture. Add the peas. When the rice is tender but still a little firm to the bite, add the Pecorino Romano cheese and butter. Stir the risotto gently until almost all of the liquid has been absorbed. Remove from the heat and allow to stand for 5–7 minutes. Top with Parmigiano-Reggiano and parsley and serve immediately.

Lobster Scallop Ragout

The Elora Mill Inn, Elora
Recommended: Henry of Pelham Family Estate Barrel Fermented Chardonnay
Makes 4 servings

This recipe is inspired by the fabulous lobster ragout made at the Elora Mill Country Inn, where it is served with handmade mustard spaetzle, tiny noodle-like dumplings. This variation on that theme can be served over rice or fettuccine, or spooned into baked puff pastry shells.

2 lb (1 kg) uncooked lobster tails
8 Tbsp (120 mL) butter
12 medium-sized scallops
1 ½ cups (5 oz/155 g) sliced button
   mushrooms
1 cup (250 mL) whipping cream

2 tsp (10 mL) Dijon mustard
salt and freshly ground black pepper
   to taste
1 ½ cups (5 oz/155 g) baby spinach,
   washed and dried

Extract the meat from the lobster tails and chop into small pieces. Melt 4 Tbsp (60 mL) of the butter in a large frying pan over medium heat. Add the scallops and cook for 45 seconds on each side. Remove and keep warm.

Melt the remaining 4 Tbsp (60 mL) butter and add the lobster meat. Cook until tender, about 3–5 minutes. Remove and keep warm.

Add the mushrooms to the pan and cook until tender, about 5 minutes. Add the cream, mustard, salt and pepper and combine well. Bring to a boil and then reduce to a simmer and cook until the sauce thickens slightly.

Return the lobster and scallops to the pan and add the spinach. Serve when the lobster and scallops are heated through and the spinach is wilted, about 1 minute.

Smoked Haddock with Scalloped Potatoes

Sam Jakes Inn, Merrickville
Recommended: Cave Spring Cellars Chardonnay Reserve
Makes 4 servings

The chef at Sam Jakes finishes this dish with a balsamic vinegar reduction and finely chopped chives. If you choose to serve this as an appetizer, cut each haddock fillet in half.

6 Yukon Gold potatoes
2 cups (500 mL) half-and-half cream
2 garlic cloves, thinly sliced
salt and freshly ground black pepper
   to taste

four 6-oz (180-g) fillets of naturally
   smoked haddock
2 Tbsp (25 mL) melted butter

Preheat the oven to 300°F (150°C). Peel the potatoes and slice very thinly (use a food processor or mandolin if possible). Place in a large heavy-bottomed saucepan over medium-high heat and add the cream, garlic, salt and pepper. Toss gently to coat all the potatoes with the cream mixture. Bring to a gentle boil and cook until the cream starts to thicken. Pour into an ovenproof dish and bake for 30 minutes. If the top browns too quickly, cover with foil.

Meanwhile place the fillets in a greased shallow baking dish and brush with the melted butter. Bake for 5–7 minutes (put the fish in the oven during the last 10 minutes of cooking time for the potatoes).

To serve, spoon a portion of potatoes into the centre of each plate. Top with a haddock fillet.

Warm Salad of Baby Spinach & Glazed Spaghetti Squash with Goat Cheese & Toasted Walnuts

Eganridge Inn, Country Club & Spa, Fenelon Falls
Makes 4 servings
Recommended: Jackson-Triggs Proprietor's Select Semillon-Chardonnay

Chef Steve Moghini pairs ingredients with a European panache, as evidenced by this creative warm salad. Partnered with a good bowl of soup, it would make a complete dinner.

For the vinaigrette:

2 Tbsp (25 mL) extra virgin olive oil
1 Tbsp (15 mL) apple cider vinegar
½ tsp (2 mL) grainy mustard

1 chive, finely chopped
½ tsp (2 mL) each salt and freshly
 ground black pepper

Combine all ingredients well in a small bowl. Set aside.

For the salad:

¾ lb (375 g) spaghetti squash, halved
 and seeded
3 Tbsp (45 mL) melted butter
¼ cup (50 mL) roughly chopped
 walnuts

1 bunch baby spinach, trimmed,
 washed and dried
1 tsp (5 mL) natural honey
3 oz (75 g) goat cheese

Preheat the oven to 375°F (190°C).

Brush the inside of the squash with 2 Tbsp (25 mL) of the melted butter and season with a little salt. Arrange face down on a parchment-lined baking sheet and bake for 45–60 minutes. While the squash is still warm, transfer the pulp into a small bowl. Set aside.

Arrange the walnuts on a small baking tray and roast in the oven for about 3 minutes; watch them carefully as nuts burn easily. Remove and set aside.

Gently toss the spinach in the vinaigrette and arrange on a serving bowl or plate.

In a frying pan, combine the remaining melted butter, honey and roasted squash. Cook for a few minutes, stirring gently, until the squash is thoroughly covered in the glaze.

Place the warm squash on top of the dressed spinach. Crumble the goat cheese on top of the salad and sprinkle the toasted walnuts over top. Serve immediately.

Jackson-Triggs

Located just a few minutes from the centre of Niagara-on-the-Lake on Niagara Stone Road, the striking, contemporary Jackson-Triggs Winery offers guided tours of every aspect of the winemaking process. Visitors can also enjoy food and wine in the Tasting Gallery, and visit the gift boutique where the limited edition Jackson-Triggs Delaine Vineyard and Grand Reserve wines are exclusively sold. During the warmer months, the winery also hosts "Twilight in the Vineyard," a gourmet dinner and show package in an open-air amphitheatre. Jackson-Triggs offers a diverse collection of wines, including a Late Harvest Vidal, Cabernet-Sauvignon Shiraz and several icewines.

Napoleon of Milk-Fed Veal & Atlantic Salmon with Maple Glaze

Eganridge Inn, Country Club & Spa, Fenelon Falls
Recommended: Cave Spring Cellars Gamay Noir Reserve
Makes 4 servings

Strictly speaking, a Napoleon is a dessert based on layers of puff pastry spread with pastry cream. However, these days chefs play with the term somewhat, just as the chef at Eganridge Inn does with this wonderful dish that layers tender veal medallions with fresh salmon.

¾ lb (12 oz/375 g) milk-fed veal
    tenderloin, cut into 4 medallions
2 Tbsp (25 mL) all-purpose flour
2–4 Tbsp (25–60 mL) vegetable oil
¾ lb (375 g) Atlantic salmon fillets
    (4 fillets, about 3 oz/190 g each)
¾ cup (175 mL) dry white wine

1 shallot, finely chopped
1 Tbsp (15 mL) Ontario maple syrup
2 Tbsp (25 mL) butter
2 chives, finely chopped
salt and freshly ground black pepper
    to taste

Preheat the oven to 400°F (200°C). Season the veal medallions with salt and paper and toss in the flour, shaking off the excess. Heat a large frying pan over medium-high heat and add 2 Tbsp (25 mL) of the vegetable oil. Sear the medallions on each side until light brown. Remove the meat to a lightly greased baking tray.

Repeat the same steps for the salmon fillets, adding the remaining oil to the pan if necessary. Place the salmon on top of the veal. Bake for about 8 minutes.

While it is baking, deglaze the frying pan with the white wine. Add the shallot and simmer until the liquid is reduced by ½. Add the maple syrup, butter, chives, salt and pepper.

To serve, place a portion of veal and salmon fillet on each plate and drizzle with the wine-maple syrup reduction.

Halibut Livornese

Woodlawn Inn, Coburg
Recommended: Henry of Pelham Family Estate Pinot Blanc
Makes 4 servings

The owners of Wooodlawn have an affiliation with Livorno, a town near Pisa in Tuscany, and this is their chef's tribute to that Italian region: succulent halibut in a simple sauce of tomato and wine. Lovely served over rice or just on its own with good, crusty bread.

four halibut fillets, 6–8oz (175–250 g) each
¼ cup (50 mL) all-purpose flour
¼ cup (50 mL) olive oil
1 can (28 oz/796 mL) diced tomatoes, drained
2 garlic cloves, minced
¼ cup (50 mL) capers, drained
2 anchovy fillets, drained and minced
¼ cup (50 mL) chopped flat-leaf parsley
¾ cup (175 mL) dry white wine
¼ cup (50 mL) butter, chilled and cut into small pieces

Lightly coat the halibut fillets in flour and shake off any excess. Heat the olive oil in a large frying pan over medium-high heat. Gently place the halibut in the frying pan and pan-sear until the crust is golden brown, 2–4 minutes. Turn and continue cooking the other side until golden brown. Remove from the frying pan and set aside.

Add the tomatoes and garlic to the pan and sauté for 1 minute. Add the capers, anchovies and parsley and continue cooking for another minute, stirring and scraping up any bits from the bottom of the pan. Add the white wine and bring to a simmer. Gradually add the butter, stirring in one piece at a time.

Place a halibut fillet on each plate and pour sauce generously over each portion. Serve immediately.

Navarin of Spring Lamb

Kettle Creek Inn, Port Stanley
Recommended: Pelee Island Winery Vinedresser Merlot
Makes 6 servings

There's nothing nicer than this classic French-styled lamb stew for an early spring supper. This recipe calls for flat ale. The chef at Kettle Creek opens a can or bottle and leaves it out overnight to use the next day.

14 cups (3.5 L) lamb or beef stock

2 cups (500 mL) flat, good-quality ale, such as Smithwick's

2 lb (1 kg) spring lamb shoulder, trimmed and cut into 1-inch (2.5-cm) cubes

salt and freshly ground black pepper to taste

8 Tbsp (120 mL) butter

2 carrots, scrubbed and diced

2 onions, diced

⅓ cup (75 mL) all-purpose flour

2 tsp (10 mL) fresh thyme leaves

2 bay leaves

2 cups (500 mL) canned diced tomatoes, with juice

¼ lb (125 g) red pearl onions, blanched and skins removed

¼ lb (125 g) baby potatoes, scrubbed

¼ lb (125 g) baby turnips, peeled

¼ lb (125 g) baby carrots, scrubbed

In a medium saucepan, heat the stock and ale to a gentle simmer. Meanwhile, season the lamb with salt and pepper. In a large pan, melt 4 Tbsp (60 mL) of the butter. Brown the lamb in small batches, and transfer to a large heavy-bottomed pot. Melt the remaining 4 Tbsp (60 mL) butter in the same pan used to brown the lamb. Add the diced carrot and onion. Cook until the vegetables are beginning to brown, then stir in the flour and cook for a few minutes more. Slowly add the warmed stock mixture to the pan, whisking continuously, until all of the stock is incorporated. Add the thyme, bay leaves and tomatoes; bring to a boil. Reduce the heat to a simmer and cook for 30 minutes. Strain the sauce over the lamb and bring the mixture to a boil. Reduce the heat and simmer for 1 ½ hours. Add the pearl onions, potatoes, turnips and carrots and cook until the vegetables are tender, about another 30 minutes.

Pelee Island Winery

At 550 acres, the Pelee vineyards comprise the largest private estate in Canada. They enjoy the unique honour of having a Vintners Quality Alliance (VQA) designated viticultural area all to themselves.

Pelee Island Winery participates in the World Wildlife Fund's strict Sustainable Vineyard Practice, which includes the use of natural fertilizers and limited pesticide spraying. Situated on Pelee Island, the southernmost inhabited point in Canada, Pelee Island Winery benefits from the longest frost-free season in Ontario, as well as the highest heat units in Canada. This makes the island natural for vinifera grape growing. Pelee Winery grows several varietals, including Chardonnay, Gewürtztraminer, Vidal, Cabernet Franc, Baco Noir and Shiraz.

Despite its southern location and warm temperatures, Pelee Island Winery was the first winery in Canada to produce icewine. In 1989, Pelee produced the first-ever Canadian red icewine. German-born winemaker and president Walter Schmoranz, one of Canada's winemaking pioneers, has led Pelee Island to hundreds of awards from around the world, notably for the 2002 Cabernet Franc Ice Wine, winner of the Citadelle de France Gold Medal.

Classic Roast Rack of Spring Lamb

Ste. Anne's Country Inn & Spa, Grafton
Recommended: Strewn Winery "Three Terroir" Merlot-Cabernet Sauvignon-Cabernet Franc
Makes 2 servings

If you're looking for a simple recipe that exudes elegance for "that special some-one," this romantic dinner à deux from Chef Christopher Ennew at Ste. Anne's is definitely it. The chef says, "From start to finish, this classic dish is ready to present on a candlelit table in under an hour." Pan-roast a few small new potatoes in butter and parsley, and steam a couple of handfuls of thin green beans to go with it.

For the lamb:
1 tsp (5 mL) Dijon mustard
¼ tsp (1 mL) honey
2 Tbsp (25 mL) vegetable oil

1 small rack of lamb (consisting of 6 chops)
pinch chopped fresh rosemary leaves

Preheat the oven to 350°F (180°C).

In a small bowl, combine the mustard and honey. Set aside.

Heat the oil over high heat in a medium-sized, ovenproof frying pan. Brown the lamb on both sides (reducing the heat if necessary, to prevent the oil from smoking). Place the lamb rack bone-side down. Turn off the heat, and coat the rack with the mustard-honey mixture. Sprinkle the rosemary over top of the mustard mixture.

Place the pan in the oven and bake for approximately 20 minutes (for medium-rare).

For the sauce:

½ small red onion, finely diced

2 Tbsp (25 mL) dry red wine

½ cup (125 mL) beef or chicken stock

salt and freshly ground black pepper
to taste

Remove the lamb from the pan to a cutting board to rest.

Cook the onion over medium-high heat in the same pan used for the lamb. Cook for 1 minute, and then deglaze the pan with the red wine. Reduce until the liquid is almost gone, and then add the stock. Reduce by ½, and adjust the seasoning if necessary.

Spoon the sauce over the lamb when ready to serve.

Lamb Patty with Garlic Aïoli

Westover Inn, St. Marys
Makes 6 servings
Recommended: Jackson-Triggs Proprietor's Reserve Merlot

These savoury meat patties have a lovely flavour that is enhanced by the smidge of garlic aïoli that crowns each one. Pick up a package of pita breads and use the patties to make delicious burgers. At the Westover Inn, the patties are complemented by barely cooked baby arugula and deep-fried parsnip chips.

For the garlic aïoli:

2 large egg yolks
4 garlic cloves, minced
2 Tbsp (25 mL) fresh lemon juice

salt and freshly ground white pepper
to taste
¾ cup (175 mL) extra virgin olive oil

In a food processor or blender, combine the egg yolks, garlic, lemon juice, salt and pepper. With the motor running, slowly drizzle in the olive oil. Continue to blend until the mixture becomes creamy. Transfer to a bowl, cover with plastic wrap and chill in the refrigerator until ready to use.

For the patties:

2 lb (1 kg) ground lamb
1 egg
3 shallots, finely chopped
3 Tbsp (45 mL) Dijon mustard

salt and freshly ground black pepper
to taste
vegetable oil as needed for frying

Combine all the ingredients in a large mixing bowl. Use your hands to work them together, then form the meat into 6-oz (180-g) patties.

Preheat the oven to 400°F (200°C). Place a frying pan over high heat. When hot, add a little vegetable oil, swirling it around to coat the surface. Add the lamb patties, a few at a time, and sear them on one side for about 3 minutes, then flip them over and transfer the pan to the oven for 5–7 minutes for medium-rare, longer if you wish. Serve as described above.

Balsamic Marinated Salmon

The Old Mill Inn & Spa, Toronto
Recommended: Pelee Island Winery Pinot Gris
Makes 4 servings

Start preparations for this recipe a day in advance to allow the salmon to marinate. It should be served cold or at room temperature as part of a buffet or main course.

four 3-oz (75-g) fresh salmon fillets, boneless and skinless
¼ cup (50 mL) all-purpose flour
2 Tbsp (25 mL) extra virgin olive oil
1 medium onion, thinly sliced
1 cup (250 mL) balsamic vinegar

1 cup (250 mL) semi-sweet white wine (Orvietto Classico works well)
¼ cup (50 mL) raisins
1 Tbsp (15 mL) brown sugar
salt and freshly ground black pepper to taste

Dredge the salmon fillets in flour and shake off any excess. Heat the olive oil in a non-stick frying pan over medium heat and fry the salmon on both sides, until the flesh is firm and cooked and the flour crust is golden brown. Remove from the pan.

Add the onion to the pan and fry until golden. Add the vinegar, white wine, raisins, brown sugar, salt and pepper and bring to a boil. Remove the pan from the heat. When cooled, transfer the marinade to a storage container large enough to hold the marinade and salmon pieces. Place the salmon in the marinade and refrigerate for 24 hours.

To serve, place the salmon pieces on individual plates and garnish with the onions and raisins from the marinade.

Pan-Seared Salmon with Sesame & Ginger

HighFields Country Inn & Spa, Zephyr
Recommended: Jackson-Triggs Grand Reserve Riesling
Makes 4 servings

Serve this delightful spring main course with new baby potatoes tossed with a bit of butter and finely chopped green onions, and a combination of asparagus and fiddleheads.

1 Tbsp (15 mL) sesame oil	four 6-oz (175-g) salmon fillets
1 tsp (5 mL) Dijon mustard	4 Tbsp (60 mL) sesame seeds
1 tsp (5 mL) rice vinegar	lemon wedges for garnish
1 tsp (5 mL) grated fresh ginger	

Combine the sesame oil, mustard, vinegar and ginger in a medium-sized bowl. Add the salmon and coat with the marinade. Marinate for 30 minutes. Just before cooking, pat 1 Tbsp (15 mL) of the sesame seeds onto each salmon fillet

Place a large non-stick pan over high heat. When the pan is very hot, add the salmon, skin-side down. Cook for 2–3 minutes on each side.

Serve with lemon wedges.

Salmon Carpaccio

The Glenerin Inn, Mississauga
Recommended: Henry of Pelham Family Estate Cuvée Catharine Rosé Brut
Makes 6–8 appetizer servings

This preparation is inspired by the salmon carpaccio served at the Glenerin Inn. Note that the carpaccio is prepared and then frozen overnight.

1 package (approx. 455 g/1 lb) smoked salmon
juice of half a lemon
1 Tbsp (15 mL) whisky
3 Tbsp (45 mL) olive oil

3 Tbsp (45 mL) chopped fresh dill
⅛ tsp (.5 mL) sugar
¼ tsp (1 mL) pink peppercorns
freshly ground black pepper to taste

On a sheet of plastic wrap approximately 18 inches (46 cm) long, lay out the slices of smoked salmon. Arrange in a rectangle.

Squeeze the lemon juice over the salmon. Sprinkle the whisky and olive oil evenly over top. Distribute the chopped dill, sugar, pink peppercorns and pepper. Roll the salmon up tightly into a log shape and freeze overnight.

Thirty minutes before serving, remove the plastic wrap and slice the salmon crosswise very thinly. If desired, drizzle good-quality olive oil over the carpaccio before serving.

Seared Fillet of Arctic Char

Sam Jakes Inn, Merrickville
Recommended: Cave Spring Cellars Chardonnay Reserve
Makes 4 servings

Char is related to both trout and salmon and is a great alternative for fans of these fish. This recipe from the chef at Sam Jakes Inn may also be used with trout or salmon.

2 shallots, diced
2 tomatoes, diced
1 bunch fresh chervil, rinsed, dried
  and trimmed
½ vanilla pod
⅓ cup (75 mL) extra virgin olive oil

¼ cup (50 mL) dry vermouth
salt and freshly ground black pepper
  to taste
4 medium-sized arctic char fillets,
  trimmed and cut into two on the
  diagonal

In a medium-sized mixing bowl, combine the shallots and tomatoes. Separate the chervil into two equal portions and finely chop one portion. Reserve the remaining chervil for garnish.

Split the vanilla pod horizontally and scrape the vanilla seeds into the bowl containing the shallots and tomatoes. Add ¼ cup (50 mL) of the olive oil, the vermouth and salt and pepper. Stir and set aside.

Place a large heavy-bottomed frying pan over high heat. Season the fish with salt and pepper. Add the remaining olive oil to the hot pan and swirl to coat the bottom of the pan completely. Cook each fillet for 3–4 minutes on each side. Remove the pan from the heat and place the fillets on serving plates. Spoon the vanilla dressing over the arctic char, and garnish with the remaining chervil.

Poached Red Snapper in Lemon Grass Nage with Quinoa & Baby Spinach

Grail Springs Health & Wellness Spa, Bancroft
Recommended: Inniskillin Wines Riesling Reserve
Makes 8 servings

This recipe features delicate red snapper gently poached in a simple lemon grass water that must be made the night before in order to let the flavours develop. Look for the organic vegetable bouillon cubes at a store that specializes in health food and organic products.

For the quinoa:

4 cups (1 L) purified water

2 organic vegetable bouillon cubes

2 cups (500 mL) quinoa, rinsed thoroughly

Bring the water to a boil in a medium saucepan. Add the bouillon cubes and quinoa. Reduce the heat to a simmer and cook for 20 minutes, or until the quinoa is tender. Set aside.

For the red snapper:

4 stalks lemon grass, split lengthwise

2 cups (500 mL) purified water

eight 4-oz (125-g) pieces of red snapper

1 lb (450 g) organic baby spinach, blanched

In a large pot, bring the lemon grass and water to a boil. Remove from the heat and let cool overnight.

Reheat the water to a simmer. Add the red snapper and cover with a lid. Remove from the heat and let sit for 15 minutes. Transfer the red snapper to serving plates and serve with quinoa and blanched spinach.

Gewürztraminer-Steamed Mussels with Tomatoes, Shallots & Spinach in Tarragon Cream

Inn on the Twenty, Jordan
Recommended: Cave Spring Cellars Gewürtztraminer
Makes 6 servings

A favourite dish from the Inn on the Twenty. Make sure to serve lots of good crusty bread alongside.

For the tarragon cream:

1 Tbsp (15 mL) grapeseed oil
1 garlic clove, chopped
2 fresh tarragon sprigs
½ red onion, finely chopped

1 bay leaf
1 ¼ cups (300 mL) whipping cream
½ cup (125 mL) Gewürztraminer

Place a heavy-bottomed pot over low heat. Add the oil, garlic, tarragon, onion and bay leaf. Sweat the mixture for 5 minutes, or until the onion is soft. Add the cream and wine and cook for another 5 minutes. Remove from the heat and keep the contents warm by placing a lid over the pot.

For the mussels:

3 lb (1.5 kg) fresh mussels, cleaned and beards removed (discard any open mussels)
2 shallots, very finely chopped
1 Tbsp (15 mL) chopped fresh thyme leaves
2 celery stalks, trimmed and very finely chopped

1 small leek, trimmed, rinsed and very thinly sliced
¾ cup (175 mL) Gewürztraminer
3 plum tomatoes, seeded and chopped
1 cup (250 mL) baby spinach, rinsed and dried

Place a heavy-bottomed pot over high heat. Leave on the heat for a few minutes so that the pot is quite hot before adding the mussels.

In a large bowl, combine the mussels, shallots, thyme, celery and leek.

Dump the mussels into the heated pot and immediately pour in the wine; be careful, as there will be a lot of steam. Cover the pot and let cook for 1 minute. Once the mussels begin to open, add the prepared tarragon cream sauce, tomatoes and spinach. Let cook for another minute or until all the mussels have opened. Discard any that have not opened. Serve immediately.

Pan-Seared Atlantic Salmon with Sweet Pea Risotto & Curry Butter

The Oban Inn, Niagara-on-the-Lake
Recommended: Jackson Triggs Gewürztraminer
Makes 4 servings

This is our version of a flavourful entrée featured on the spring menu at the Oban Inn in Niagara-on-the-Lake. If you're preparing this out-of-season, substitute frozen peas. Serve with a fresh salad based on shaved fennel and mache (or baby spinach).

For the curry butter:

4 Tbsp (60 mL) butter	½ cup (125 mL) Chardonnay
1 Tbsp (15 mL) extra virgin olive oil	1 tsp (5 mL) fresh lemon juice
2 small shallots, finely diced	1 cup (250 mL) 35% cream
1 tsp (5 mL) curry powder	

In a saucepan, combine the butter and oil over medium heat. Add the shallots and sauté gently until they are softened; do not brown. Add the curry powder and stir into the shallot mixture, cooking for another minute. Now add white wine and lemon juice and stir well together. Bring the mixture to a gentle boil and cook until thickened and reduced slightly. Add the cream and continue to boil gently until thickened and reduced by ½. Remove from heat and whisk in the butter. Season with salt and pepper and keep warm.

For the risotto:

1 cup (250 mL) peas, fresh or frozen	1 onion, finely chopped
5–6 cups (1.5 L) vegetable, fish or chicken stock (approx.)	2 cloves garlic, minced
	2 cups (500 mL) arborio rice
¼ cup (50 mL) extra virgin olive oil	½ cup (125 mL) Chardonnay
2 Tbsp (25 mL) butter	

In a pot of lightly salted, boiling water, cook the peas for 2 minutes. Drain and refresh under cold running water; drain and set aside.

In a large saucepan, bring the stock to a boil. Reduce heat and keep stock at a steady simmer throughout the rest of the cooking.

In a heavy-bottomed saucepan, heat the olive oil and butter over medium-high heat. Add the onion and cook for 2 minutes or until translucent. Stir in the garlic and cook for 2 minutes. Add the rice all at once; cook, stirring, for 2 minutes or until grains are coated with butter and oil. Pour in the wine; cook, stirring, for 1 minute or until the wine is absorbed.

Using a ladle, start to add simmering stock ½ cup (125 mL) at a time. As each ladle of stock is added, stir the rice to keep it from sticking to the bottom and sides of the pan; do not add more until the last addition is absorbed. If the stock is absorbed too quickly, reduce the heat to maintain a slow, steady simmer. Repeat this process, ladling in the hot stock and stirring, for 15 minutes. As you near the end of the cooking time, reduce the amount of stock to ¼ cup (50 mL) at a time.

Stir in the peas and continue to cook, adding more stock as necessary until the rice is tender but with a firm heart and overall creaminess. Keep warm while you prepare the salmon.

For the salmon:

3 Tbsp (45 mL) olive oil	four 7-oz (220 g) Atlantic salmon fillets
salt and freshly ground pepper	

Warm the oil in a frying pan over fairly high heat. Season the salmon and place in the hot pan. Sear the salmon for about 5 minutes on one side; then, using a metal spatula, flip the salmon and cook for another 1–2 minutes. (Alternatively you may sear the salmon in the hot pan until golden brown, then finish cooking to desired doneness in a 375°F/190°C oven.)

Place a portion of risotto in a warm, shallow soup or pasta plate. Top with a portion of salmon and curry butter. Serve immediately.

Main Courses
Summer

Summertime and the living is at its absolute easiest when you choose to spend it at an Ontario country inn. Whether visitors plan on a weekend away or much longer, the pleasures of the summer season are magnified and made even more memorable in these beautiful settings. Summer theatre, cycling, hiking, boating, golf, winery tours and tastings, water sports or just time spent lounging in a beautiful outdoor setting, all of these and so much more are waiting to be discovered. After an activity-filled day outdoors, there is nothing nicer than the anticipation of an aromatherapy massage, facial, or one of any number of spa therapies at your resident inn. Refreshed, rejuvenated and relaxed, your day draws to a close but not before a splendid dinner comprised of locally grown foods, creatively prepared, and a glass or two of fine Ontario wine. Summer at the inn—a quintessential Canadian experience.

Chapter Four

Lamb Satay with Peanut Sauce

The Waring House Inn, Picton
Recommended: Inniskillin Wines Gamay Noir
Makes 6 servings

You can use chicken, beef or pork in this recipe—just make sure to use tender cuts of meat. Traditionally, the meat for satays is cut into thin strips and threaded onto skewers, but in this recipe the lamb is cut into cubes before being threaded onto water-soaked wooden skewers. The peanut sauce is a Malaysian-style sauce that works well with any meat; make it a day ahead to allow the flavours to develop. It will keep for up to a week, covered, in the refrigerator. Lastly, be sure to shake the can of coconut milk well before opening.

For the peanut sauce:

2 Tbsp (25 mL) vegetable oil
1 onion, finely chopped
2 garlic cloves, minced
½ tsp (2 mL) crushed red pepper flakes
¼ cup (50 mL) fresh lime juice

¼ cup (50 mL) light soy sauce
⅔ cup (150 mL) natural, crunchy
   peanut butter
⅓ cup (75 mL) coconut milk
¼ cup (50 mL) chopped cilantro

In a small, heavy saucepan, warm the oil over medium heat. Add the onion, garlic and pepper flakes; cook for 8 minutes or until the onion and garlic are soft and golden. Add the lime juice, soy sauce, peanut butter and coconut milk. Stir to blend well; cook until heated through. Remove from the heat; stir in the cilantro, and set to one side.

For the lamb satay:

2 lb (1 kg) boneless lamb, cut into
    1-inch (2.5-cm) pieces
1 inch (2.5 cm) fresh ginger, peeled
    and grated
2 Tbsp (25 mL) soy sauce
2 Tbsp (25 mL) vegetable oil
1 tsp (5 mL) turmeric

1 tsp (5 mL) smoked paprika
2 garlic cloves, minced
2 Tbsp (25 mL) light brown sugar
2 Tbsp (25 mL) fresh lime juice
1 tsp (5 mL) ground coriander
1 tsp (5 mL) chili powder

Place the lamb pieces in a bowl. Combine all the remaining ingredients in a smaller bowl and whisk together to blend. Pour this mixture over the lamb pieces, rubbing it well into the meat. Cover with plastic wrap and let marinate 8 hours or overnight, refrigerated.

Soak 6 wooden skewers in water for 1 hour. Remove the lamb from the refrigerator half an hour before grilling.

Preheat the grill to high. Thread the lamb onto the water-soaked wooden skewers. Grill the satays for 2 minutes per side or until cooked through, turning often. Serve with the peanut sauce.

Scallops with Black Pudding & Pancetta with Cayenne Hollandaise

The Elora Mill, Elora
Recommended: Strewn Winery Chardonnay Terroir American Oak
Makes 4 servings

This is an elegant summer dish that pairs seared scallops and rounds of black pudding (rich blood sausage) with a little crispy bacon. Fresh salad greens accompany and a little lustrous hollandaise is drizzled over for a striking visual effect. If you are not fond of black pudding (although, when it is well-made, as it is in the Elora region, it is an excellent product), substitute any good-quality, full-flavoured sausage. The chef recommends making the hollandaise sauce first and keeping it warm while you prepare the rest of the recipe. The secret to making hollandaise (you can do it) is patience. Just remember to keep the egg yolks at a minimal even heat as you add the melted butter. If you suddenly find it curdling, remain calm, add a big fat ice cube and keep whisking until it has melted.

For the hollandaise sauce:

3 large egg yolks	¾ cup (175 mL) melted butter
¼ tsp (1 mL) cayenne	salt and white pepper to taste
1 ½ Tbsp (22 mL) white wine vinegar	

Place a medium-sized saucepan half-filled with water over high heat. Bring to a boil, then reduce the heat to allow the water to boil gently. Place the eggs, cayenne pepper and vinegar in a stainless steel bowl and whisk to blend. Place the bowl over the saucepan of simmering, not boiling, water and continue to whisk vigorously until the mixture is light. Occasionally remove the bowl from over the water to allow the mixture to cool (you don't want to scramble the eggs). When you can lift the whisk and see that the eggs have reached the ribbon stage (as the chef describes it, "if you lift the whisk out of the egg mixture and you could write with the mixture"), remove the bowl from the saucepan and very slowly whisk in the melted butter. You must do this very slowly or the sauce will curdle and separate. Once all the butter has been incorporated, add the salt and pepper, cover the bowl with plastic wrap and set to one side. Don't refrigerate or keep hot; it should be at room temperature when you serve it.

For the scallops:

4 cups (1 L) mixed salad greens
5 Tbsp (75 mL) olive oil
12 medium-sized scallops
salt and freshly ground black pepper
  to taste
12 slices black pudding or other
  sausage, about ½ inch (1.2 cm)
  thick

1 shallot, minced
2 garlic cloves, minced
½ cup (125 mL) white wine
6 oz (180 g) pancetta (unsmoked
  bacon), chopped and cooked until
  crisp

Place the salad greens in a large mixing bowl and toss together with 1 Tbsp (15 mL) of the olive oil and a bit of salt and pepper. Set to one side.

Place a large frying pan over high heat and allow to get very hot. Season the scallops with salt and pepper on both sides, add the remaining olive oil to the pan and place the scallops in the pan. Leave the scallops to sear, undisturbed, for approximately 45–60 seconds, then turn them over and sear on the other side. Add the black pudding to the pan. After 30 seconds turn the black pudding slices over, then turn the scallops over again. Add the shallot and garlic to the pan along with the white wine. Allow to come to a boil, and when almost all the wine has evaporated, remove from the heat and set aside.

To serve, place some of the greens on each of 4 plates. Arrange 3 black pudding slices in 3 points around each plate. Place a scallop on each slice of black pudding. Spoon some of the hollandaise on top of each scallop and garnish each with a little crisped pancetta.

Grilled Vegetable Tower with Parsley Pesto

The Elora Mill Inn
Recommended: Pelee Island Winery Sauvignon Blanc
Makes 4 servings

Filled with the flavours of summer, this is served at Elora Mill as part of their Sunday brunch during the hot summer months. It works well as a main course and also as a starter for grilled chicken, pork or lamb. Vary the vegetables as different varieties become available throughout the summer and early fall. If you wish, add slices of warmed goat cheese to the finished dish.

For the parsley pesto:

1 large bunch flat-leaf parsley, rinsed
4 garlic cloves, crushed
1 cup (250 mL) grated Parmesan
cheese

1 tsp (5 mL) salt
½ tsp (2 mL) freshly ground black
pepper
½ cup (125 mL) extra virgin olive oil

Place the parsley and garlic in a food processor or blender and pulse until finely minced. Add the cheese, salt, pepper and olive oil and purée until the mixture is smooth. Transfer to a small bowl and set aside.

For the grilled vegetables:

1 small eggplant, trimmed and sliced
crosswise
1 red bell pepper, halved and seeded
1 green bell pepper, halved and
seeded
1 large red onion, peeled and cut into
wedges
1 large zucchini, sliced lengthwise

4 portobello mushrooms, wiped clean,
black gills and stems removed
(discard gills; reserve stems for
another use)
olive oil as needed
coarse salt and freshly ground black
pepper to taste

Place all the vegetables in a large bowl and toss with enough olive oil to make them glisten. Season with salt and pepper. Preheat the grill to medium-high. Grill the vegetables, brushing them with olive oil as they cook, until just tender and lightly charred. Depending on the vegetable, this could take 6–15 minutes. Don't overcook.

To serve, place a portobello cap on each serving plate. Drizzle each with parsley pesto, top with pieces of the remaining vegetables (in any order you wish), with a little drizzle of parsley pesto in between each, and end with a little more of the pesto at the finish. Serve immediately.

Grilled Pickerel Cheeks

The Kettle Creek Inn, Port Stanley
Recommended: Colio Estate Wines CEV Pinot Grigio
Makes 4 servings

If you've never experienced pickerel cheeks—a specialty of the Lake Erie region—you're in for a real treat. At the Kettle Creek Inn, in the picturesque fishing village of Port Stanley, pickerel cheeks are a staple of the menu, when in season. While they're readily available in this area, if you have trouble obtaining them elsewhere, you can still put this recipe together using other fish fillets, such as tilapia, perch or trout. Or visit the inn's dining room and enjoy them there where they're often teamed with a beet tartar sauce and a drizzle of chive oil. Once you've sampled them, you'll also want to try dipping the cheeks in egg and breadcrumbs and shallow-frying them. The following preparation is also quite nice served over pasta.

1 lb (500 g) pickerel cheeks, washed well	2 Tbsp (25 mL) extra virgin olive oil
juice of 2 limes	2 Tbsp (25 mL) chopped fresh chives
salt and freshly ground black pepper to taste	1 Tbsp (15 mL) chopped fresh tarragon
	lemon wedges for garnish

Soak 4 bamboo skewers in water. Place the pickerel cheeks in a shallow non-reactive dish large enough to hold them all in one layer. In a small bowl, whisk together the lime juice, olive oil, salt, pepper and fresh herbs. Pour this mixture over the pickerel cheeks, lifting them up to allow the marinade to flow beneath the fish. Cover with plastic wrap and marinate for 2 hours in the refrigerator. Preheat the grill to medium-high.

Carefully thread the pickerel onto the skewers. Place on the hot grill and cook for approximately 1–2 minute per side (depending on the size of the cheeks). Transfer to a serving platter and garnish with lemon wedges.

Adzuki Bean Burger

Ste. Anne's Country Inn & Spa, Grafton
Recommended: Henry of Pelham Family Estate Baco Noir
Makes 8 servings

Here is a typical spa recipe from Ste. Anne's Chef Christopher Ennew. Adzuki beans are russet-coloured beans with a slightly sweetish flavour. The dried beans can be purchased whole at Asian foodshops or health-food outlets. Serve these patties on a bed of greens or as you would a traditional burger.

2 lb (1 kg) adzuki beans, cooked
2 Tbsp (25 mL) tahini (sesame seed
    paste)
3 Tbsp (45 mL) minced garlic
2 Tbsp (25 mL) extra virgin olive oil
salt and freshly ground black pepper
    to taste

3 Tbsp (45 mL) chopped fresh parsley
2 Tbsp (25 mL) chopped fresh mint
2 Tbsp (25 mL) chopped fennel
    (discard the root)
¼ cup (50 mL) vegetable oil

Place the beans in the food processor along with the tahini, garlic and olive oil. Process using the on/off switch until the mixture is relatively smooth. Scrape the mixture into a bowl and add the seasoning, fresh herbs and fennel. Shape into 8 patties. Warm the oil in a frying pan over medium-high heat and fry the patties until crispy on the outside and heated through, turning once, about 6 minutes in total.

Crusted Sea Bass with Pickled Vegetable Salad

Sir Sam's Inn & WaterSpa, Haliburton
Recommended: Jackson-Triggs Proprietor's Grand Reserve Chardonnay
Makes 4 servings

This dish calls for panko, Japanese breadcrumbs that are coarser than those sold in most supermarkets. They help to give the fish a lovely, crusty coat. Look for them in shops or markets that specialize in Asian products. (We have also had very good results coating fish fillets with potato flakes.) Start by making the vegetable salad. Take the time to properly cut the vegetables into classic julienne —very thin, matchstick-like strips, about 3 inches (7.5 cm) long.

For the salad:

1 celery stalk, trimmed and julienned

1 carrot, scraped and julienned

1 red onion, julienned

2 leeks, trimmed, rinsed and julienned
(white part only)

1 seedless cucumber, peeled and
julienned

juice of 1 large lemon

coarse salt and freshly ground black
pepper to taste

Place all the salad ingredients in a bowl, toss together well, cover with plastic wrap and refrigerate for 2–3 hours. Remove the salad from the refrigerator 30 minutes before serving.

For the fish:

¼ cup (50 mL) black sesame seeds,
toasted

½ cup (125 mL) panko

four 6-oz (175-g) skinless sea bass
fillets

1 tsp (5 mL) lemon pepper seasoning

2 eggs, lightly beaten in a shallow
bowl with 1 Tbsp (15 mL) water

2 tsp (10 mL) vegetable oil

1 tsp (5 mL) butter

lemon wedges and dill for garnish

Place the sesame seeds in a shallow bowl and the breadcrumbs in another. Season the fish with some of the lemon pepper seasoning. Dip each fillet in the egg wash, then the sesame seeds, then the breadcrumbs, patting the toppings to keep them in place and transferring the fillets to a tray while you work. Preheat the oven to 350°F (180°C).

Place a medium-sized frying pan on medium heat. Add the oil and butter. When the butter has melted, add the fish fillets (work with one or two at a time) and sear for 1 minute. Use a wide spatula to carefully turn the fish over and sear the other side for another minute. When all the fillets have been seared, transfer the tray to the preheated oven and cook for an additional 4 minutes. The fish should just begin to flake when touched.

To serve, place the fish on warm plates and top with the pickled salad. Garnish with fresh lemon wedges, dill or cilantro.

Black Bean & Sautéed Onion Salsa

Ste. Anne's Country Inn & Spa, Grafton
Makes 3 cups (720 mL)

The chef recommends serving this interesting salsa with your favourite corn chips or as a condiment with grilled vegetables, chicken or pork. Or stir some of it into cooked rice for a quick side dish. Make the sautéed onions ahead of time, and allow enough time for the flavours of the salsa to develop.

1 Tbsp (15 mL) olive oil
1 cup (250 mL) cooked black beans
1 shallot, finely diced
1 small green bell pepper, seeded
    and diced
2 garlic cloves, minced

2 Tbsp (25 mL) red wine vinegar
1 cup (250 mL) diced tomato
salt and freshly ground black pepper
½ cup (125 mL) sautéed onions
3 lengths of cilantro, chopped

Heat the olive oil in a saucepan. Add the shallots and cook until softened, about 4 minutes. Add the green pepper and garlic and cook for another 3 minutes. Add the vinegar and let the mixture cook until the vinegar is mostly reduced. Add the tomatoes and bring to a boil. Add the black beans. Reduce the heat and let simmer for 10 minutes. Season with salt and pepper. Add the sautéed onions and chopped cilantro, and stir to incorporate all ingredients. Cover with plastic wrap and let stand for an hour or so before using.

Grilled Lamb Sausage with Tabbouleh Salad

The Briars Resort & Spa, Jackson's Point
Recommended: Colio Estate Wines CEV Meritage
Makes 6–8 servings

Make the grain salad ahead of time to allow the flavours to develop. Serve with grilled pita bread.

For the tabbouleh salad:

⅔ cup (150 mL) bulghur

¼ cup (50 mL) finely sliced green onions

2 cups (500 mL) coarsely chopped flat-leaf parsley

¼ cup (50 mL) chopped mint

1 large ripe tomato, diced

¼ cup (50 mL) thinly sliced radish

¼ cup (50 mL) extra virgin olive oil

⅓ cup (75 mL) fresh lemon juice

generous pinch salt

¼ tsp (1 mL) freshly ground black pepper

Pour the bulghur into a medium-sized bowl, add just enough cold water to cover and soak for 30 minutes. Line a sieve with cheesecloth and pour the bulghur into it. Gather the cheesecloth together and squeeze tightly to remove all the water. Discard the water. Return the bulghur to the bowl. Add the remaining ingredients to the bulghur and toss so that all the ingredients are well combined. Cover with plastic wrap and refrigerate until ready to serve. Remove from the refrigerator about 15 minutes before serving.

For the sausage:

8 large, lean lamb sausages

Preheat the grill to high. Place the sausages on the grill, close the lid or cover with a foil tent. Grill the sausages, turning often, until lightly browned, about 10 minutes in total.

To serve, spoon the tabbouleh salad onto a serving platter and arrange the sausages over top.

Herb-Crusted Beef Tenderloin

Sir Sam's Inn & WaterSpa, Haliburton
Recommended: Cave Spring Cellars Cabernet Merlot
Makes 15 servings

Reserve this fantastic summer entrée from Sir Sam's Inn for a time when you have a crowd to feed. Use a cast-iron pan to sear the beef and then finish the cooking on the grill or barbecue in the same pan. Start preparing this at the beginning of the day.

For the beef:

5–6-lb (2.2–2.7-kg) whole beef
   tenderloin, silver skin removed
4 cups (1 L) vegetable oil
6 garlic cloves, chopped
¼ cup (50 mL) roughly chopped fresh
   thyme leaves
¼ cup (50 mL) roughly chopped
   fresh basil
¼ cup (50 mL) roughly chopped
   fresh sage
juice and zest of 3 oranges

Place all the ingredients in a shallow dish. Turn the beef, turning to coat all sides. Cover with plastic wrap and refrigerate for 6–8 hours.

For the herb crust:

4 cups (1 L) dried breadcrumbs
¼ cup (50 mL) chopped fresh thyme
   leaves
¼ cup (50 mL) chopped fresh basil
¼ cup (50 mL) chopped fresh rosemary
   leaves
¼ cup (50 mL) crushed garlic
¼ cup (50 mL) fresh flat-leaf parsley
   leaves
1 Tbsp (15 mL) salt
1 Tbsp (15 mL) freshly ground black
   pepper
2 Tbsp (25 mL) olive oil

Pour the breadcrumbs into a large mixing bowl. Combine the herbs, salt and pepper in the bowl of a food processor. Purée until blended. Scrape the mixture into the breadcrumbs, add the olive oil and toss to mix well. Scatter this mixture over the surface of a baking tray. Set aside.

Preheat the grill to medium-high. Remove the beef from the marinade (discard the marinade) and pat dry. Place a large cast-iron pan over high heat. Add a little olive oil and sear the beef on all sides until browned. Remove the beef from the pan and place on the breadcrumb mixture. Roll the meat around to thoroughly coat all sides with the breadcrumb mixture. Return to the cast-iron pan and transfer to the grill rack. Close the lid and roast the meat for 30–40 minutes, checking to make sure the temperature gauge does not go above 350°F (180°C). If it does, open the grill cover. (Alternatively, roast the meat in the oven.) Let the meat rest for 15 minutes before slicing and serving.

Grilled Beef Tenderloin with Asparagus & Tomato Risotto

The Briars Resort & Spa, Jackson's Point
Recommended: Henry of Pelham Family Estate Baco Noir
Makes 4 servings

Chef Trevor Ledlie, executive chef at The Briars, suggests making the balsamic jus the day before to help with preparation. The risotto will take a bit of planning but the results are well worth it. (Get the barbecue expert in your house to handle grilling the steaks while you concentrate on the risotto.) Note that the asparagus and zucchini need a little precooking. Any leftover risotto is wonderful the next day shaped into small patties and fried in a little butter or oil. Look for white balsamic vinegar in supermarkets or specialty food shops.

For the balsamic jus:

2 cups (500 mL) white balsamic vinegar

1 cup (250 mL) chicken stock

½ cup (125 mL) light brown sugar

1 garlic clove, smashed

Combine all the ingredients in a large saucepan over medium heat. Bring to a boil and allow to reduce by ½. Remove the garlic and discard and set the balsamic jus to one side.

For the risotto:

2 Tbsp (25 mL) butter

2 Tbsp (25 mL) extra virgin olive oil

1 large red onion, diced

1 bay leaf, fresh or dried

2 garlic cloves, minced

½ tsp (2 mL) minced jalapeño pepper

2 cups (500 mL) arborio rice

2 cups (500 mL) dry white wine

5 cups (1.25 L) hot chicken stock

1 lb (500 g) asparagus, trimmed, blanched and cut into ¼-inch (.6 -cm) pieces

1 yellow zucchini, diced and blanched

4 plum tomatoes, seeded and diced

(ingredients continue next page)

1 tsp (5 mL) truffle oil (optional)

1 tsp (5 mL) chopped fresh thyme
leaves

1 tsp (5 mL) white balsamic vinegar

½ cup (125 mL) grated Grana Padano
or Parmesan cheese

salt and freshly ground black pepper
to taste

In a large, heavy saucepan over medium heat, melt the butter with the oil. Add the onion, bay leaf and garlic. Cover the pan and cook for 2 minutes, stirring once or twice. Stir in the rice and sauté, stirring constantly, for 2 minutes. Add the wine, stirring it into the mixture. When the first bubbles appear, add 1 cup (250 mL) of the hot chicken stock and the balsamic vinegar, stirring while the liquid is absorbed. Repeat this procedure, adding ½ cup (125 mL) of the chicken stock at a time until the risotto is creamy but still a little *al dente*. (You may not need all of the stock.) Set to one side. (You will complete the risotto after the beef is cooked.)

For the beef:

four 6-oz (180 g) beef tenderloin   salt and freshly ground pepper to taste

Preheat the grill to high. Place the beef tenderloin on the grill, close the lid and sear the meat for 2 minutes per side (sear for 3–4 minutes if the tenderloins are thicker than 1 inch/2.5 cm). Reduce the heat to medium and continue to cook to the desired doneness. Let the beef rest for 10 minutes before serving.

To serve, gently reheat the risotto if necessary. Reheat the balsamic jus. Add the asparagus and zucchini to it, along with the remaining butter, jalapeño, chopped tomato, truffle oil (if using), thyme and cheese. Fold these ingredients into the risotto. Place a portion of risotto on a serving plate and lay a beef tenderloin over top.

Creole Catfish BLT with Cajun Mayonnaise

The Vintage Goose Inn & Spa, Kingsville
Recommended: Pelee Island Winery Monarch Vidal
Makes 2–3 servings

A variation on the well-known and popular BLT sandwich, this version from the Vintage Goose Restaurant includes a few crunchy fillets of catfish in its ingredient list. Pickerel or perch fillets would probably also work quite well. If you find the combination of fish and peameal (back) bacon a little too hearty, omit the bacon. Look for "Cajun seasonings" in the spice section of your supermarket. Start by making the mayonnaise first.

For the Cajun mayonnaise:

½ cup (125 mL) good-quality
    store-bought mayonnaise
2 Tbsp (25 mL) Cajun seasonings

juice and zest of 1 lemon
salt and freshly ground black pepper
    to taste

Combine the ingredients in a small bowl and whisk together to blend well. Cover with plastic wrap and refrigerate until ready to use.

For the fish:

1 cup (250 mL) yellow cornmeal
2 tsp (10 mL) cayenne pepper
1 cup (250 mL) all-purpose flour
1 cup (250 mL) whole milk (or
    half-and-half cream)

3 eggs, lightly beaten
salt and freshly ground pepper to taste
2–3 catfish fillets
3 Tbsp (45 mL) olive oil

In a mixing bowl, combine the cornmeal, cayenne pepper and flour and mix well. In another bowl, whisk together the milk and eggs. Season with salt and pepper. Dip the fish fillets in the egg and milk mixture, then into the cornmeal mixture, shaking off the excess. Transfer the coated fish to a plate as you work.

Heat the oil in a frying pan over medium-high heat. Add the fillets and cook for about 4 minutes on each side until golden and cooked through.

To serve:

1 baguette, sliced in half horizontally

3 Tbsp (45 mL) extra virgin olive oil

1 large garlic clove, halved

½ lb (250 g) thinly sliced peameal bacon, cooked

2 large tomatoes, sliced

½ head Boston lettuce, washed, dried and leaves separated

Preheat the oven to 300°F (150°C). Brush the baguette with the olive oil and rub with the garlic clove. Toast in the oven for just a few minutes until the edges of the bread are crisped.

Cover both sides of the bread with the Cajun mayonnaise. Layer 1 side with the bacon, tomato and lettuce. Place the fried catfish on the other side and place both halves together. Slice into 2 or 3 servings and serve at once.

Roma Tomato Tart with Asiago & Parmesan

The Glenerin Inn, Mississauga
Recommended: Colio Estate Wines CEV Cabernet Franc Reserve
Makes 4–6 servings

This pretty summer tart from the dinner menu at Glenerin is a convenient preparation as it is easily made in advance. This version of their recipe makes one large tart; however, at the Glenerin they make individual tarts based on puff pastry. Either way it's delicious.

1 prebaked 9-inch (23-cm) pie crust
¼ cup (50 mL) grated Asiago cheese
¼ cup (50 mL) grated Parmesan
   cheese
20 basil leaves, roughly torn
4–5 plum tomatoes, sliced ⅛ inch
   (.3 cm) thick

3 Tbsp (45 mL) olive oil
1 garlic clove, finely chopped
salt and freshly ground black pepper
   to taste

Preheat the oven to 350°F (180°C). Sprinkle both cheeses on the bottom of the pie crust. Scatter ½ the basil leaves over the cheese. Arrange the slices of tomato in an attractive overlapping pattern. Drizzle the olive oil over the tomatoes and scatter garlic over all. Season with salt and pepper. Bake for about 10–15 minutes, until the tomatoes are cooked and the tart is warmed through. Remove from the oven and let sit for 15 minutes before serving. Serve each slice with some of the remaining torn basil leaves and a drizzle of extra virgin olive oil.

Grilled Wellington Portobello Mushrooms

The Waring House Inn
Recommended: Inniskillin Wines Pinot Noir Reserve
Makes 4 servings

Chef Luis de Sousa says this is one of the Inn's most popular appetizers.

For the chive oil:

1 bunch chives, chopped
6 green onions, trimmed and chopped
(green part only)

1 cup (250 mL) vegetable oil

Place the chives, green onions and vegetable oil in a food processor bowl and blend until smooth. Pour into a plastic squeeze bottle and refrigerate.

For the mushrooms:

4 portobello mushrooms, wiped
clean, black gills discarded and
stems removed (reserve stems for
another use)
1 Tbsp (15 mL) balsamic vinegar
½ cup (125 mL) goat cheese, softened

3 Tbsp (45 mL) extra virgin olive oil
2 Tbsp (25 mL) diced red bell pepper
2 slices prosciutto, chopped
freshly ground black pepper to taste
4 cups (1 L) mixed baby greens, lightly
dressed with a bit of olive oil

Preheat the grill to high. Grill the mushrooms until they're soft and slightly grill-marked. Line a baking tray with parchment paper. Combine the vinegar and oil in a bowl. As the mushrooms are cooked, dip them in the mixture. Place the mushrooms, cavity side up, on the tray. Set to one side.

Preheat the oven to 400°F (200°C). Combine the goat cheese, red pepper, prosciutto and black pepper. Cream the mixture and divide evenly into four small patties. Place one in the centre of each mushroom cap. Bake for 5–8 minutes until the cheese is beginning to melt. Serve on a bed of dressed baby greens and drizzle the chive oil around the edges.

Chipotle Cornish Hen on Boston Lettuce with Buttermilk & Chive Dressing

Inn on the Twenty, Jordan
Makes 6 servings
Recommended: Cave Spring Cellars Pinor Noir

The perfect summer recipe that involves smearing little Cornish hens with a vibrant chipotle-based rub. Chipotle chiles are smoked jalapeño peppers that are usually sold in cans packed in adobo sauce. Make sure to include some of the sauce along with the chipotle itself. This paste would also work well on chicken, pork or salmon. Start by making the salad dressing and the paste. Note: it will be far easier to grill the birds if you flatten them before you apply the paste. Turn the bird breast-side up and press down on it with the palm of your hand. Apply some pressure to break a few of the rib bones. Alternatively, if you have a spit roaster on your barbecue, use it to cook the birds.

For the salad:

1 cup (250 mL) buttermilk

3 Tbsp (45 mL) chopped fresh chives

¼ tsp (1 mL) chopped fresh cilantro

1 Tbsp (15 mL) liquid honey

salt and freshly ground black pepper to taste

3 heads Boston lettuce, washed and dried thoroughly

Combine the buttermilk, chives, cilantro, honey, salt and pepper in a small bowl (or a jar with a lid) and blend together well. Refrigerate the dressing for at least an hour. Wash and thoroughly dry the lettuce, wrap in a clean tea towel and refrigerate.

For the Cornish hens:

1 tsp (5 mL) chopped fresh thyme leaves

2 Tbsp (25 mL) garlic purée

salt and freshly ground black pepper to taste

2 Tbsp (25 mL) grapeseed oil

3 Tbsp (45 mL) chipotle chiles

1 tsp (5 mL) chopped fresh chives

¼ tsp (1 mL) chopped fresh sage

6 Cornish hens

Using a mortar and pestle, blend the thyme, garlic, salt, pepper, oil, chipotle, chives and sage together to form a paste. Alternatively, use a food processor or blender and scrape the mixture into a bowl.

Rub some of the spice paste well into each of the Cornish hens. Place the hens on a tray and cover with plastic wrap. Refrigerate for 2–3 hours. Remove the hens from the refrigerator 30 minutes before grilling.

Preheat the grill to medium-high. Set a foil drip tray beneath the grill. Cook the hens for 10 minutes and then turn. Continue cooking, turning every 10–15 minutes, for a total of about 40 minutes or until the juices run clear. Let rest for 15 minutes before serving.

Arrange the lettuce on a large serving platter (or individual serving plates). Drizzle with salad dressing and arrange the Cornish hens over the salad. Pass round any remaining dressing at the table.

Main Courses
Fall

Local colour takes on a whole new meaning when we think of autumn in Ontario. It's difficult to avoid invoking clichés when describing the beauty of fall in this province. This is a time of the year when people from all over Canada, and the world, head to the region to explore the natural wonder of autumn in the province. Fall also brings its own culinary style, with inn menus that include game, mushrooms, rich sauces and the beginning of the slow-cooked season with heartier fare. It's all here in the special recipes of autumn from Ontario's Finest Inns.

Chapter Five

Pinot Noir-Braised Pheasant
with Potato Gnocchi

The Old Mill Inn & Spa, Toronto
Recommended: Henry of Pelham Speck Family Reserve Pinot Noir
Makes 4 servings

You don't often see pheasant on modern dining room menus these days and that's too bad. When cooked properly, young pheasant can be a wonderful treat. This classic preparation can be used with guinea fowl or chicken as well. Make the fabulous potato gnocchi ahead of time and reheat.

For the potato gnocchi:

3 floury potatoes, peeled and quartered	¼ tsp (1 mL) freshly grated nutmeg
salt to taste	1 ½ cups (375 mL) all-purpose flour
2 eggs, lightly beaten	¼ cup (50 mL) grated Parmesan cheese

Place the potatoes in a saucepan, cover with cold salted water and bring to a boil. Cook the potatoes until tender, about 25 minutes. Drain, reserving the cooking water. Transfer the potatoes to a bowl and let cool. Add the eggs and nutmeg and mash well. Gradually add the flour and Parmesan and combine with the potato mixture to form a dough; you may not use all the flour or you may need a little more. Turn the dough out onto a lightly floured surface and knead lightly for 2 minutes until smooth.

Divide the dough into 4 pieces and roll each one into a long, cylindrical shape. Using the edge of a fork, cut each length into 1-inch (2.5-cm) pieces. Use the tines of the fork to lightly flatten each piece, leaving an impression. Repeat with the remaining dough.

Return the potato cooking water to the heat and add a little more water to it. Bring to a boil and drop each gnocchi into the water; they will sink to the bottom and then rise. Don't crowd the pot—you may have to cook the gnocchi in two batches. Once they rise, let them continue to cook for about 1 minute. Remove the gnocchi with a slotted spoon and keep warm while you prepare the pheasant.

For the pheasant:

6 Tbsp (90 mL) unsalted butter
3 ½ lb (1.6 kg) pheasant pieces,
   breast and leg
¾ cup (175 mL) chopped celery
¾ cup (175 mL) chopped carrot
1 onion, chopped
6 slices double-smoked bacon,
  chopped

2 garlic cloves, chopped
1 ½ cups (375 mL) Pinot Noir
1 ½ cups (375 mL) chicken stock
2 bay leaves
4 fresh thyme sprigs
½ cup (125 mL) tomato paste
salt and freshly ground white pepper
  to taste

In a large frying pan over medium-high heat, melt the butter. When it is foaming, add the pheasant pieces and cook on both sides until golden brown, about 8 minutes. Transfer to a platter.

Add the celery, carrot, onion, bacon and garlic to the pan and cook, stirring the mixture together until the onion begins to brown and the bacon is cooked, about 12 minutes. Add wine and use a wooden spoon to deglaze the pan by scraping up all the bits on the bottom as the wine reaches boiling point. Add the chicken stock, bay leaves, thyme and tomato paste, stirring to blend. Season with salt and pepper and transfer the pheasant pieces and any accumulated juices back to the pan, nestling the pieces into the sauce. Slowly simmer the pheasant for about 35–40 minutes or until tender. Transfer to a platter.

Bring the liquid back to a boil and boil gently until reduced by ½. Place a sieve over a bowl and pour the mixture through the sieve, pressing the solids against the sides to force as much of the sauce through the sieve as possible; don't forget to scrape the underside of the sieve, too. Discard the solids and return the sauce to the pan along with the pheasant pieces. Heat everything through for a minute or two and serve immediately with the gnocchi.

Red Chile-Crusted Filet Mignon with Chipotle Mushroom Sauce

Trinity House Inn, Gananoque
Recommended: Jackson-Triggs Proprietor's Reserve Pinot Noir
Makes 4 servings

Strictly for heat seekers, spiced-and-seared steaks are smothered in a full-bodied mushroom sauce influenced by more chile heat, modified by the creaminess of yogurt and the sweetness of honey. Unusual and very good. Start by making the sauce.

For the chipotle mushroom sauce:

2 Tbsp (25 mL) olive oil

½ medium-sized red onion, finely diced

1 large garlic clove, finely chopped

2 cups (500 mL) dry red wine

½ lb (250 g) cremini mushrooms, wiped clean and sliced ¼ inch (.6 cm) thick

3 cups (750 mL) chicken stock

½ lb (250 g) portobello mushrooms, wiped clean and sliced ¼ inch (0.6 cm) thick

2 Tbsp (25 mL) finely chopped canned chipotle (with its sauce)

2 Tbsp (25 mL) honey

2 Tbsp (25 mL) plain yogurt

salt and freshly ground black pepper to taste

In a large saucepan over medium-high heat, warm the oil. Sauté the onion and garlic until softened and fragrant, about 5 minutes or so. Add the wine, increase the heat to high and let the mixture boil until most of the liquid has evaporated, about 15–20 minutes or so. Reduce the heat and add all the mushrooms, stirring them into the mixture. Add the stock, bring the mixture to a boil, then reduce the heat to allow everything to simmer for about 15 minutes. Whisk in the chipotle and cook for another 5 minutes. Add the honey, yogurt, salt and pepper and continue to cook for a minute to blend the flavours. Use immediately or set to one side to reheat when the steaks are ready.

For the steaks:

2 Tbsp (25 mL) chili powder

½ tsp (2 mL) paprika

½ tsp (2 mL) red chili flakes

1 Tbsp (15 mL) cracked black
peppercorns

1 Tbsp (15 mL) brown sugar

salt to taste

4 filet mignons

3 Tbsp (45 mL) olive oil

Combine all the chili powder, paprika, chili flakes, peppercorns, sugar and salt together in a small bowl. Stir to blend well. Pour the spice mixture onto a plate. Dredge each steak just on one side with the spice mixture, pressing it well into the meat.

Place a large pan on high heat. When hot, add the olive oil and, when almost smoking, place the steaks spice-side down in the pan. Sear the steaks until a crust forms, about 2–3 minutes or so. Use tongs to turn the meat over, reduce the heat to medium and continue to cook the meat for 3–4 minutes more or until cooked to your liking. Let sit for a minute or two before serving with the chipotle mushroom sauce.

Vintner's-Style Venison with Spaetzle

Eganridge Inn, Country Club & Spa, Fenelon Falls
Recommended: Henry of Pelham Family Estate Merlot Unfiltered
Makes 4 servings

These days farm-raised game meats like venison and elk are widely available to the home cook. Many are lower in fat than conventional meats, not to mention full of flavour and quick to cook—as this simple, but impressive main course from Chef Steve Moghini proves. Make the spaetzle ahead of time; they are not at all difficult to make. You can use a spaetzle press, available at cookware shops, or do what many chefs do and force the dough through a large-holed colander to form the little noodle-like dumplings. If you prefer, serve the venison with store-bought pasta of your choice or rich, homemade mashed potatoes. This main course comes together in less time than you'd imagine.

For the spaetzle:

3 cups (750 mL) all-purpose flour
1 tsp (5 mL) salt
dash ground nutmeg
dash ground white pepper

4 eggs
¾ cup (175 mL) water
3 Tbsp (45 mL) melted butter

Place a sieve over a mixing bowl and into it sift the flour, salt, nutmeg and pepper into the bowl. In another smaller bowl, whisk together the eggs and water; add to the flour mixture. When the mixture starts to get thick, beat with a wooden spoon until smooth. Continue beating the dough until it is elastic and gelatinous, about 2–3 minutes. Let the dough rest for an hour before proceeding.

Bring a large pot of water to a boil over high heat. Place the butter in a pan over low heat. Place the spaetzle press or colander over the boiling water, add the dough and press the dough into the water. When the spaetzle float to the surface, they are cooked. Using a slotted spoon, remove to the pan with the melted butter and keep warm.

164

For the venison:

1 ¼ lb (625 g) lean venison, trimmed
   and cut into medallions

salt and freshly ground black pepper
   to taste

flour for light dredging

3 Tbsp (45 mL) olive oil

1 large shallot, finely chopped

20–30 red seedless grapes

1 Tbsp (15 mL) grainy mustard

½ cup (125 mL) dry red wine

1 cup (250 mL) demi-glace or rich beef
   stock

¼ cup (50 mL) whipping cream

Season the medallions with salt and pepper and lightly dredge with flour, shaking off the excess. Place a large frying pan over medium-high heat and when hot, add the olive oil. When it is almost smoking, add the medallions and sear on each side for just 1 minute each. Transfer the medallions to a warm platter and keep warm.

In the same frying pan, sauté the shallot for a few minutes, then add the grapes and the mustard. Add the wine and deglaze the pan, scraping up any bits clinging to the bottom of the pan and allowing the mixture to cook away until the liquid has been reduced a little and the mixture has a syrup-like consistency. Add the demi-glace or stock and the cream; bring to a gentle boil. Season with salt and pepper. Keep quite warm.

To serve, toss the spaetzle to coat with butter. Transfer a portion to a warm plate and top with a portion of venison and sauce.

Olive & Herb-Crusted Rack of Lamb

Woodlawn Inn, Cobourg
Recommended: Pelee Island Winery Vinedresser Cabernet Sauvignon
Makes 4 servings

The menu at the Woodlawn reflects a European sensibility as evidenced by this impressive main course of rack of lamb with a Provence-like influence. A good butcher will be happy to french the lamb racks for you. Start by making the tapenade. Serve with skinny green beans tossed in a little butter and a creamy potato gratin.

For the tapenade:

¼ cup (50 mL) pitted black kalamata olives

1 Tbsp (15 mL) capers, drained
2 Tbsp (25 mL) extra virgin olive oil

In a food processor, combine the olives and capers. Pulse until small pieces are formed. With the motor running, add ½ the olive oil in a drizzle, and continue to process until a rough paste forms. Scrape the mixture into a small bowl and set aside.

For the lamb:

1 rack of Ontario lamb (2–2½ lb/ 1–1.3 kg) frenched and split in half (4 chops each half)
salt and freshly ground black pepper to taste
½ cup (125 mL) seasoned dry breadcrumbs

2 Tbsp (25 mL) extra virgin olive oil
1 shallot, minced
½ tsp (2 mL) coarse-grained mustard
1 tsp (5 mL) jarred mint sauce
⅛ cup (25 mL) dry red wine
¼ cup (50 mL) whipping cream

Preheat the oven to 375°F (190°C). Place a large frying pan over high heat. Season the lamb with salt and pepper. When the pan is hot, add the remaining olive oil and, just as it begins to smoke, sear the lamb racks fat-side down until a golden-brown crust forms, about 5 minutes or so.

Use tongs to turn the racks over, and slather them first with the olive tapenade and then the breadcrumbs. Slip the pan into the oven for 10–12 minutes (this will produce medium-rare lamb; recommended). Return the pan to the stovetop and place over medium heat. Remove the lamb to a warm platter and let rest 6–8 minutes. Meanwhile, add the shallot, mustard and mint sauce to the pan and cook for 1 minute, stirring to blend. Deglaze the pan with the red wine, scraping up all the bits clinging to the bottom. Add the cream and simmer for 1 minute. Adjust the seasoning. Slice each lamb rack in ½ between the ribs and transfer to a serving plate. Serve the sauce over the lamb.

Grilled Pork Tenderloin with Celery Root Fritters, Braised Red Cabbage & Carrot Reduction

Westover Inn, St. Marys
Recommended: Henry of Pelham Family Estate Baco Noir
Makes 4–6 servings

A lovely presentation for fall menus, this complete dinner entrée from the chefs at the Westover Inn may be produced in its entirety or you may choose to make one or two of the components to go with other preparations. The celery root fritters would be lovely served with oven-baked fish or sautéed chicken, and the cabbage-apple mixture is great with sausages, ham or roast pork. The vibrant carrot reduction makes a great base or topping sauce for fish like halibut or tilapia, pan-seared scallops, chicken or an array of grilled vegetables. The original recipe for the carrot reduction called for almost a pound (500 g) of butter! This is a lighter version that is quite full-flavoured thanks to fresh orange juice, chicken stock and a bit of ginger. Be sure to read this entire recipe through before you begin. Start by making the cabbage mixture, then the carrot reduction, followed by the celery root fritter mixture and finally the pork tenderloin.

For the red cabbage:
2 ½ Tbsp (32 mL) butter
½ red cabbage, cored and thinly sliced
1 ½ tsp (7 mL) salt

2 Granny Smith apples, peeled, cored and diced

In a frying pan over medium heat, melt the butter. Add the cabbage, apples and salt and sauté over low heat for approximately 1 ½ to 2 hours, stirring frequently. (If necessary, add a very little water from time to time to prevent the mixture from sticking.) Cover and set aside.

For the carrot reduction:

3 carrots, peeled and chopped

juice of 2 oranges

1 cup (250 mL) chicken stock

1 tsp (5 mL) freshly grated ginger

¼ cup (50 mL) butter, chilled and diced

salt and freshly ground black pepper
to taste

Place the chopped carrots, orange juice and chicken stock in the bowl of a food processor. Use the on/off button to pulse the mixture until blended. Transfer to a saucepan, place over high heat, and cook for about 10 minutes until it is reduced by ½ and begins to coat the back of a spoon. Stir in the ginger and remove from the heat. Use a whisk to blend in the butter a little at a time. Season with salt and pepper, then pass the mixture through a fine sieve. Set to one side.

For the celery root fritters:

1 lb (500 g) celery root, peeled and cut
into small chunks

3 large Yukon Gold potatoes, peeled
and cut into small chunks

½–1 cup (125–250 mL) all-purpose
flour

salt and freshly ground black pepper
to taste

¼ cup (50 mL) grated Parmesan
cheese

1 egg, slightly beaten

vegetable oil for deep-frying

salt to taste

In a large saucepan, combine the celery root and potato chunks. Add salt and water to just cover, and bring to a boil over high heat. Reduce the heat to medium and cook for about 15–20 minutes or until the vegetables are soft. Drain well and put the vegetables through a ricer (or just mash thoroughly). Add the flour, salt, pepper, Parmesan and egg; mix everything together well.

(continues on next page)

Heat the oil to 300°F (150°C) in a deep-fryer or other heavy-based pot. (The accuracy of the oil temperature is vital, so if you are not using a deep-fryer with a gauge, use a candy thermometer to determine the temperature of the oil.) Using 2 tablespoons, shape the fritter batter into small oval shapes (called quenelles), transferring them to a tray as you work. Add the quenelles to the hot oil, a few at a time. Fry them until golden brown, turning them around in the fat to encourage even colouring. Remove with a slotted spoon to a paper towel-lined tray and salt them while still hot. Place in a warm oven.

For the pork:

1–2 pork tenderloins (1 ½–2 lb /
   750 g–1 kg)
1 Tbsp (15 mL) chopped fresh thyme
   leaves

salt and freshly ground black pepper,
   to taste

Trim the tenderloins of any silver skin (very thin membrane that may be covering it) with a sharp knife, removing as little meat as possible. Combine the thyme, salt and pepper in a small bowl, mix thoroughly, then rub well into the meat. Preheat the grill to medium-high. Cook the tenderloins for 20–25 minutes in total, or to the desired doneness. (You could also pan-fry or oven-roast the meat.) Remove from the heat and let rest for 6 minutes tented loosely with foil to keep warm. Slice the meat on the diagonal.

To serve, pour some of the carrot reduction on a plate. Arrange the meat over the sauce, and place a portion of the cabbage mixture next to it. Finally, add 2 or 3 fritters to the plate and serve immediately.

Mushroom-Crusted Veal Tenderloin with Calvados

Ste. Anne's Country Inn & Spa
Recommended: Inniskillin Meritage Reserve
Makes 4 servings

If you have difficulty obtaining veal tenderloin, substitute pork tenderloin or boneless chicken breasts. Serve with root vegetables and whole cranberry sauce.

1 cup (250 mL) dried mushrooms, crushed
1 ¼ lb (625 g) veal tenderloin
2 tsp (10 mL) olive oil
2 cups (500 mL) veal or chicken stock
1 shallot, finely minced
salt and freshly ground white pepper to taste
⅛ cup (30 mL) Calvados

Place the crushed mushrooms in a food processor, blender or spice grinder and grind until fine. Transfer to a plate and roll the tenderloin in the dried mushrooms. Wrap the meat in plastic wrap and refrigerate for 2 hours.

When ready to cook, preheat the oven to 350°F (180°C). Place a frying pan over high heat. When hot, add 1 tsp (5 mL) of the oil, swirl it around and place the tenderloin in the pan, searing on all sides for a minute or two in total. Transfer the pan to the oven and cook for 10–12 minutes.

While the meat is cooking, pour the veal or chicken stock into a saucepan, place over high heat and boil until reduced by ½. In a small saucepan, heat the remaining 1 tsp (5 mL) oil, add the shallot, salt and pepper and sauté for a few minutes until softened. Deglaze the pan with the Calvados, scraping up any bits from the bottom. Add the reduced stock to the pan and stir to blend well. Cook until slightly reduced, then reduce the heat to a simmer.

Remove the tenderloin from the oven and let rest for 5 minutes before slicing and serving with the sauce.

Salmon with Bacon & Red Wine Sauce

The Breadalbane Inn, Fergus
Recommended: Inniskillin Wines Gamay Noir
Makes 4 servings

Chef Paul Torrance and the busy kitchen brigade at Breadalbane Inn are responsible for the meals served in the two dining rooms and also prepare the classic Scottish pub fare served in the adjacent Fergusson Room Pub. This seasonal specialty dish is from the main dining room menu. Serve it with small, new potatoes and a green vegetable.

four 6-oz (180-g) salmon fillets
2 Tbsp (25 mL) olive oil
salt and freshly ground black pepper
  to taste
¼ lb (125 g) double-smoked bacon,
  diced

1 ½ cups (375 mL) dry red wine
salt and freshly ground black pepper
  to taste
3 Tbsp (45 mL) chopped fresh parsley

Preheat the oven to 275°F (135°C). Place a baking sheet on the centre rack. Rub the salmon all over with the olive oil and season with salt and pepper. Set aside.

Place a medium-sized saucepan over medium heat and cook the bacon until crisp. If there is a lot of fat, drain off a portion, leaving about 2 Tbsp (25 mL). Remove from the heat and set aside.

Heat a large heavy frying pan (cast iron is good) until it is searingly hot (the hotter the better). Working with 2 fillets at a time, add the salmon to the hot pan, skin-side down and cook without disturbing the fish until the skin is very crisp, about 2 minutes. Turn the fillets over and continue to cook for another 2–3 minutes until crisp and golden brown (longer if you prefer it well done). Remove from the pan and transfer to the oven to keep warm while you cook the remaining salmon.

Return the saucepan holding the bacon to the heat, add the wine and bring to a boil, cooking until the liquid is reduced and slightly thickened. Season with salt and pepper.

Transfer the salmon to a warmed serving platter and spoon the sauce over each piece. Sprinkle with parsley and serve immediately.

Muskoka Cranberry Elk

Inn at the Falls, Bracebridge
Recommended: Inniskillin Wines Braeburn Estate Vineyard Shiraz
Makes 4 servings

There are two major cranberry-growing areas in Muskoka and the yearly Bala Cranberry Festival is a much-anticipated event in the region. It's logical, then, for this Bracebridge inn to team local farm-raised elk with the cranberries for which the area is renowned. Demi-glace is quite time-consuming for the home cook to prepare, but you can purchase it at food shops and upscale food markets. While the actual cooking of the elk loin is quite brief, allow plenty of time for the meat to marinate. The chef recommends serving this with roasted garlic mashed potatoes, sections of sweet potato or a selection of grilled vegetables. Start by making the sauce.

For the sauce:

½ cup (125 mL) fresh cranberries
2 Tbsp (25 mL) granulated sugar

½ cup (125 mL) Cabernet-Merlot or
    other dry red wine
1 cup (250 mL) demi-glace

Place the cranberries in a heavy-based medium-sized saucepan. Cover with the sugar and cook over medium heat, breaking the cranberries up slightly with a wooden spoon. Reduce the heat a little and continue to cook until the cranberries are slightly caramelized, about 12 minutes or so. Add the red wine, bring the mixture to a boil and cook at a gentle boil until the wine is reduced by ½, about 12 minutes more. Add the demi-glace and continue to cook until the mixture has thickened, another 10 minutes or so. Set aside and keep warm.

For the elk:

1 tsp (5 mL) garlic purée

½ cup (125 mL) Cabernet-Merlot or
    other dry red wine

pinch coarse salt

2-lb (1-kg) boneless elk loin, sliced
    ¼ inch (.6 cm) thick

2–3 Tbsp (25–45 mL) olive oil

In a shallow dish, whisk together the garlic, wine and salt. Place the elk slices in the marinade, turning it over once or twice to coat the meat. Cover with plastic wrap and refrigerate for 3 or 4 hours. Remove from the refrigerator at least 30 minutes before cooking.

Remove the elk from the marinade and pat dry with paper towels. Place a sauté pan on high heat. Add 2 Tbsp (25 mL) of the olive oil to the pan, swirl it around, and then add the elk pieces and sear quickly on both sides. Don't crowd the pan; do this in stages if the pan is not large enough. Cook for a total of about 2 minutes per side for medium-rare (the recommended cooking time for elk). Serve with the cranberry sauce.

Irish Beef & Guinness Stew with Garlic Mashed Potatoes

The Westover Inn, St. Marys
Recommended: Colio Estate Wines CEV Merlot Reserve
Makes 4–6 servings

A classic stew that will be much anticipated as the weather changes from cool to cold. Put the potatoes on to boil in the last 30 minutes of cooking time for the stew. If you don't have a casserole dish with a fitted lid, a large piece of aluminum foil tucked tightly around the top of the dish will work just as well.

For the stew:

2 lb (1 kg) stewing beef, trimmed and cut into 2-inch (5-cm) cubes

3 Tbsp (45 mL) vegetable oil

2 Tbsp (25 mL) all-purpose flour

salt and freshly ground black pepper to taste

pinch cayenne

2 large white onions, coarsely chopped

1 garlic clove, crushed

2 Tbsp (25 mL) tomato paste, dissolved in ¼ cup (50 mL) water

1 ½ cups (360 mL) Guinness

2 cups (500 mL) carrots, peeled and coarsely chopped

1 cup (250 mL) parsnips, peeled and coarsely chopped

1 fresh thyme sprig

Preheat the oven to 300°F (150°C).

Toss the meat with 1 Tbsp (15 mL) of the oil to coat. In a separate bowl, combine the flour, salt, pepper and cayenne. Toss the meat in the flour mixture to coat thoroughly.

Heat the remaining oil in a large frying pan over medium-high heat. When the oil is hot, add the beef, turning to brown it on all sides. Reduce the heat and add the onions, garlic and tomato paste. Cover the frying pan and gently cook for 5 minutes.

Transfer the meat to a large casserole dish with a slotted spoon.

Pour ½ the Guinness into the frying pan. Bring to a boil and stir to dissolve the caramelized meat juices from the pan. Pour over the meat, along with the remaining Guinness.

Add the carrot, parsnip and thyme to the casserole dish, stirring gently to mix thoroughly. Adjust the seasoning to taste. Cover the casserole dish and bake for 2 to 3 hours, until the meat is tender.

For the garlic mashed potatoes:

2 lb (1 kg) floury potatoes (such as Yukon Gold), peeled and quartered

1 tsp (5 mL) salt

1 head garlic, separated into cloves and peeled

½ cup (125 mL) butter

½ cup (125 mL) whipping cream

¾ cup (175 mL) whole milk (approximately)

Place the quartered potatoes in a medium-sized saucepan and just cover with cold water. Stir in the salt. Cover the saucepan loosely and place over high heat. Bring to a boil and then reduce the heat to medium. Add the garlic cloves to the water. Put the lid on completely and boil gently for about 20 minutes. When the potatoes are tender all the way through, remove them and the garlic from the heat and drain, keeping them in the saucepan. Turn off the heat and return the potatoes to the burner, shaking the pot back and forth a few times until all residual moisture has disappeared. Leave the pot on the burner and add the butter, mashing well. Gradually add the cream and milk, mashing well after each addition. Once all the cream and milk has been added, tilt the pot to one side and, using a flat whisk or wooden spoon, stir the potatoes quickly to incorporate some air into the mash. When creamy and fluffy, cover the mash with a clean cloth and pot lid until ready to serve with the stew.

Cider-Braised Chicken with Mushrooms & Apples

Gananoque Inn, Gananoque
Recommended: Cave Spring Cellars Chardonnay CSV
Makes 4 servings

It would be difficult to find a recipe with more autumn appeal than this one from Chef Erik Seiffert. This is one from the Inn's cooking school repertoire. Start by preparing the mushroom stock. The stock uses the stems from the mushrooms, so remove them and set the mushrooms aside for the next step. This dish is very nice served over rice or pasta with a simple green salad alongside.

For the mushroom stock:

1 lb (500 g) assorted mushrooms
   (shiitake, oyster, cremini etc.),
   wiped clean
1 medium-sized onion, peeled and
   coarsely chopped
1 carrot, coarsely chopped
1 stalk celery, coarsely chopped

½ tsp (2 mL) black peppercorns
1 bay leaf
1 clove
2 cups (500 mL) water
salt and freshly ground black pepper
   to taste

Remove the stems from the mushrooms. Slice the mushroom caps and set aside. Combine the stems in a medium-sized pot with the onion, carrot, celery, peppercorns, bay leaf, clove and water. Bring the stock to a boil, reduce the heat and simmer for 30 minutes. Season with salt and pepper. Strain, discard the solids and set aside.

For the chicken:

4 skinless, boneless chicken breasts, cut into 1-inch (2.5-cm) pieces
salt and freshly ground black pepper to taste
4 Tbsp (60 mL) olive oil
1 medium onion, finely chopped
1 cup (250 mL) apple cider

2 Tbsp (25 mL) apple cider vinegar
1 Granny Smith apple, peeled, cored and coarsely chopped
2 Tbsp (25 mL) chopped fresh rosemary
2 Tbsp (25 mL) all-purpose flour
2 Tbsp (25 mL) honey

Season the chicken with salt and pepper. Heat 2 Tbsp (25 mL) of the olive oil in a heavy saucepan over medium-high heat. Add the chicken pieces and sauté until brown on all sides, about 5 minutes. Transfer the chicken to a plate. Place the remaining olive oil in the saucepan. Add the reserved sliced mushroom and the onion and sauté for 2–3 minutes. Add ¼ cup (50 mL) of the apple cider to the saucepan and bring to a boil, deglazing the pan and scraping up any bits clinging to the bottom of the pan. Let the liquid boil until reduced to only 2 Tbsp (25 mL). Return the chicken to the pan and stir in the apple and rosemary. Sprinkle the flour over all and stir to coat evenly. Slowly stir in 1 cup (250 mL) of the mushroom stock, apple cider vinegar, honey and remaining ¾ cup (175 mL) apple cider. Bring to a boil, reduce the heat and simmer for 30 minutes, stirring occasionally. Taste and season with salt and pepper if desired and serve. (This dish can be made a day ahead. Cool slightly, refrigerate uncovered until cold, then cover and keep chilled. Reheat before serving.)

Curry-Scented Lamb Burger with Ratatouille & Cheddar

Inn on the Twenty, Jordan
Recommended: Cave Spring Cellars Cabernet Merlot
Makes 6 servings

How to elevate the humble burger—add lean ground lamb to the mix, top it with the colourful, delicious vegetable mélange known as ratatouille and sharp cheddar, and serve it up on a quality bun. Start by making the ratatouille.

For the ratatouille:

2 Tbsp (25 mL) olive oil
½ eggplant, trimmed and diced
1 green zucchini, trimmed and diced
1 yellow zucchini, trimmed and diced
1 red pepper, seeded and diced
1 red onion, peeled and diced

½ fennel bulb, trimmed and diced
1 garlic clove, minced
2 Tbsp (25 mL) capers
2 plum tomatoes, seeded and diced
salt and freshly ground black pepper
 to taste

In a heavy saucepan over high heat, heat the oil and quickly sauté all ingredients except the tomatoes. Cook for about 5 minutes, stirring to encourage even cooking, then remove from the heat. Stir the tomatoes into the mixture and season with salt and pepper. Set aside.

For the burger:

2 lb (1 kg) lean ground lamb
1 lb (500 g) regular ground beef
2 cups (500 mL) panko (Japanese
 breadcrumbs)
1 Tbsp (15 mL) mild curry paste
1 tsp (5 mL) Dijon mustard
1 tsp (5 mL) garlic powder

2 tsp (10 mL) finely chopped green
 onion
2 tsp (10 mL) chopped fresh basil
salt and freshly ground black pepper
6 oz (180 g) aged cheddar cheese,
 sliced
6 good-quality buns

Combine the meat, breadcrumbs, curry paste, mustard, garlic powder, green onion, basil, salt and pepper in a mixing bowl and mix together thoroughly, using your hands. Shape the mixture into 6 patties. Grill the patties over medium heat, about 3–4 minutes per side, or to desired doneness. During the last minute or two, top each patty with a slice of cheddar. Serve on the buns and top with ratatouille.

Wellington Wild Mushroom Fricassee

Merrill Inn, Picton
Recommended: Pelee Island Winery Pinot Noir
Makes 2 servings

A quick-to-make little dish that never fails to please, this mushroom sauté can be easily doubled to serve another two people. Chef Michael Sullivan pairs this earthy combination with smoked duck in a fresh herb and balsamic reduction. You can serve this mixture over hot, buttered toast (our favourite), or as an appetizer paired with mixed greens.

2–4 Tbsp (25–60 mL) butter
6 large white mushrooms, wiped clean and sliced into large pieces
6 large shiitake mushrooms, wiped clean and sliced into large pieces
1 large portobello mushroom, wiped clean and sliced into large pieces
1 tsp (5 mL) minced shallot
1 small garlic clove, minced
2 tsp (10 mL) finely chopped fresh tarragon

½ tsp (2.5 mL) finely chopped fresh parsley
½ ripe tomato, peeled, seeded and diced
1 green onion, trimmed and thinly sliced on the bias
salt and freshly ground black pepper to taste
½ tsp (2 mL) fresh lemon juice

In a large sauté pan over high heat, melt the butter. When foaming and just starting to brown, add all the mushrooms and immediately toss to coat each mushroom lightly with butter. Cook for 3–4 minutes, stirring the mushrooms occasionally. Add additional butter as needed to keep the bottom of the pan constantly coated with butter. When the mushrooms have browned and are cooked through, add the shallot, garlic and fresh herbs. Cook briefly for about 30 seconds and add the tomato and green onion. Season with salt, pepper and the lemon juice, stirring to blend, and serve hot.

The dining room at Sir Sam's Inn & WaterSpa

Domain of Killien

Lamb Patty with Garlic Aïoli, Westover Inn (p. 124)
Photo by Sean Camp, Lucid Musings Photography

Napoleon of Milk-Fed Veal & Atlantic Salmon,
Eganridge Inn, Country Club & Spa (p. 118)

Porch at Trinity House Inn

The Little Inn of Bayfield

Grail Springs Health & Wellness Spa

Fresh Mixed Berries in a Phyllo Cup
Ste. Anne's Country Inn & Spa (p. 225)

HighFields' Harvest Vegetable Strudel

HighFields Country Inn & Spa
Recommended: Inniskillin Wines Servos Vineyard Viognier
Makes 4 servings

There is always a main course vegetarian option at HighFields Inn, where Chef Mark Mogensen puts his years of spa-styled cooking to very good use. The chef recommends serving this savoury pastry with a salad or lightly wilted greens. You will need to prepare the squash and peppers ahead of time.

2 cups (500 mL) baked, mashed
    squash (butternut works well)
2 cups (500 mL) julienne of assorted
    vegetables: carrot, celery root,
    leeks, parsnip
1 large red bell pepper, roasted and
    seeded

1 Tbsp (15 mL) chopped fresh basil
1 tsp (5 mL) grated fresh ginger
1 tsp (5 mL) vinegar
½ tsp (2 mL) salt
8 sheets phyllo dough
cooking spray
2 egg whites, whisked

Preheat the oven to 350°F (180°C). In a mixing bowl, combine the squash, julienned vegetables, bell pepper, basil, ginger, vinegar and salt. Mix together gently.

Lay out 4 sheets of phyllo and lightly spray each sheet with cooking spray. Place a second sheet on top of each sheet and lightly spray with cooking spray. Brush the top of each stack with a little egg white.

Divide the filling into 4 portions. Place a portion along the short edge of each of the 4 sheets. Do not go right to the edge and do not spread it out right to the sides; leave about 2 inches (5 cm) at each side. Fold the edges toward the middle over the filling and then roll the strudel up. Place on a baking sheet with the seam side down. Give each of the rolls a light spray with the cooking spray.

Bake for 25–35 minutes or until lightly browned. Serve immediately.

Roasted Pork Tenderloin with Rosemary Pesto & Prosciutto

The Waring House Inn, Picton
Recommended: Jackson-Triggs Delaine Vineyard Cabernet Merlot
Makes 4–6 servings

This favourite of the cookery school instructor is easy and very good with a nice glass of Chardonnay. Serve with steamed rice or noodles tossed in a little butter and fresh green beans.

1–2 pork tenderloins (1 ½–2 lb/
   750 g–1 kg)
2 Tbsp (25 mL) freshly chopped
   rosemary leaves
2 garlic cloves, minced

1 anchovy fillet
¼ cup (50 mL) olive oil
fresh cracked black pepper to taste
6–8 slices prosciutto

Trim the tenderloins of any silver skin (very thin membrane that may be covering it) with a sharp knife, removing as little meat as possible. Make a pesto by combining the rosemary, garlic, anchovy, oil and pepper in a mortar and using the pestle to grind the mixture to a fine paste. Rub onto the pork and let sit for 30 minutes (or cover with plastic wrap and refrigerate overnight).

Preheat the oven to 400°F (200°C). Lay a piece of ovenproof plastic wrap (the chef suggests the Handi-Wrap brand) on a work surface. Place the prosciutto on the wrap, overlapping the slices. Place the pork tenderloin on top of the prosciutto and roll up. Place the roll seam-side down on a baking sheet and roast in the oven for 15 minutes or until cooked to your liking. Remove from the oven and let rest for 10 minutes, covered. Remove the plastic wrap, and slice and serve as described above.

Gamay Noir-Poached Beef Tenderloin

Sam Jakes Inn, Merrickville
Recommended: Colio Estate Wines Gamay Noir
Makes 6 servings

This special presentation for a special dinner from Sam Jakes Inn features top-quality Canadian Angus beef, gently simmered in Colio Estates Gamay Noir. The chef teams the beef with sautéed bell peppers and crisp straw potatoes.

2 Tbsp (25 mL) olive oil
4 shallots, finely chopped
6 black peppercorns
1 bay leaf
1 bottle (750 mL) Colio Estate Gamay Noir

six 6-oz (170-g) beef tenderloins, trimmed
salt and freshly ground black pepper to taste
8 Tbsp (100 mL) butter

In a large saucepan, warm the olive oil over medium-high heat. Add the shallots and sauté, along with the peppercorns and bay leaf, until the shallots are beginning to caramelize, about 10 minutes or so. Set to one side.

Pour the wine into a large frying pan and gently warm over medium heat until the wine is just simmering. Slip the tenderloins into the wine and very gently poach the beef for 4 minutes, for rare, another minute or two for medium-rare. It is very important that the wine is very gently simmering, not boiling. Transfer the cooked beef from the frying pan to a warm platter. Loosely tent with foil to keep warm.

Add the poaching wine to the saucepan holding the shallots. Place over high heat and boil rapidly until the liquid is reduced by ⅔, about 15 minutes. Season with salt and pepper. Strain the reduced liquid into a smaller saucepan and keep warm over a low heat. Whisk in the butter, 1 Tbsp (15 mL) at a time until the mixture is glossy and thickened. Spoon the sauce over and around each tenderloin and serve immediately.

Wild Mushroom Farfalle

Gananoque Inn, Gananoque
Recommended: Inniskillin Wines Montague Estate Vineyard Pinot Noir
Makes 4 servings

Simple and delicious, this comforting mushroom and pasta dish is quick to prepare. Serve as a prelude to roast pork or chicken or as a main course preceded by a salad of peppery greens.

¼ cup (50 mL) olive oil
1 lb (500 g) assorted wild mushrooms
   (shiitake, chanterelle, oyster),
   stems removed, caps wiped clean
   and chopped
salt and freshly ground black pepper
   to taste

½ cup (125 mL) Marsala
2 cups (500 mL) whipping cream
½ cup (125 mL) chopped fresh parsley
1 lb (500 g) farfalle pasta
2 tsp (10 mL) salt
1 cup (250 mL) grated Parmesan
   cheese

Put a large pot of water on to boil over high heat and cover with a lid. Place a medium-sized pan over high heat. Allow the pan to get quite hot, then add the olive oil, mushroom caps, salt and pepper. Sauté the mushrooms until they are almost cooked through, about 3–5 minutes. Add the Marsala and cook for about 30 seconds to reduce the liquid. Add the cream and parsley. Reduce the heat slightly and let the mixture cook until the sauce has reduced and thickened, about 6 minutes or so. Meanwhile, cook the pasta with the salt in a pot of boiling water until tender but still firm to the bite, about 6–7 minutes. Drain well, then add the pasta to the mushrooms and toss together. Serve in warmed bowls and sprinkle Parmesan over each serving.

Main Courses
Winter

Every season brings its unique rewards. This maxim is truly, and perhaps most magically, experienced during Canada's winter months. After a day spent hiking over snow-covered trails or skiing the slopes, there are few experiences more comforting and restorative than the hearty, warming entrées you may expect to enjoy at Ontario's Finest Inns.

Chapter Six

MAIN COURSES—WINTER

Roast Pork Loin with Red Wine Sauce & Apple Compote

Lantern Inn, Port Hope
Recommended: Henry of Pelham Family Estate Cabernet Baco
Makes 6 servings

This very involved, quite rich dish features pork stuffed with black pudding. This modified version leaves out the black pudding, and adds roasted potatoes. You'll need a roasting pan fitted with a rack for this recipe.

For the roast pork:

2 Tbsp (25 mL) whole black peppercorns

6 branches rosemary, leaves only, finely chopped

1 Tbsp (15 mL) coarse salt

3 lb (1.5 kg) boneless loin of pork

1 Tbsp (15 mL) whole cloves (optional)

2 ½ –3 lb (1.25–1.5 kg) potatoes, peeled and cut into large chunks

6 garlic cloves, smashed

1 Tbsp (15 mL) olive oil

½ tsp (2 mL) salt

¼ tsp (1 mL) freshly ground black pepper

Preheat the oven to 425°F (220°C).

With a mortar and pestle, crack the peppercorns. (Or wrap the peppercorns in a tea towel and smash with a kitchen mallet or rolling pin until cracked.) Mix the peppercorns with the chopped rosemary and salt; press the mixture all over the surface of the roast. If using cloves, insert them randomly into the roast. Set the roast aside.

Toss the potatoes with the garlic, olive oil, salt and pepper. Fit a roasting pan with a rack and place the potatoes around the rack. Roast for about 30 minutes.

Reduce heat to 375°F (190°C). Place the roast on the rack and roast the meat and potatoes for about 1 ½ hours. Meanwhile, prepare the compote.

For the apple compote:

1 cinnamon stick

2 whole cloves

1 star anise

¼ cup (50 mL) butter

3 McIntosh apples, peeled, cored and diced

⅓ cup (75 mL) granulated sugar

Wrap the spices in a small square of cheesecloth and tie with kitchen twine. Set aside.

Melt the butter in a medium-sized frying pan over medium-high heat. Add the diced apples and spice bag and reduce the heat to medium. Add the sugar and cook until the apples are soft, but not falling apart. Remove from the heat and discard the spice bag.

For the red wine sauce:

2 Tbsp (25 mL) olive oil

1 small onion, finely chopped

2 garlic cloves

⅔ cup (160 mL) sliced white mushrooms

1 fresh thyme sprig

2 cups (500 mL) red wine

1 ½ cups (375 mL) beef stock

¾ tsp (4 mL) grainy mustard

Heat the olive oil over medium-high heat. Sauté the onion, garlic, mushrooms and thyme until golden brown. Add the red wine and reduce by three-quarters. Add the beef stock and simmer over low heat for 20–30 minutes, until the sauce has thickened.

Just before plating the roast pork and potatoes, gently reheat the compote. Slice the pork and drizzle the red wine sauce over top. Serve with the potatoes and warmed apple compote.

Grilled Black Angus with Upper Canada Dark Ale & Dijon Mustard Sauce

The Westover Inn, St. Marys
Recommended: Colio Estate Wines CEV Merlot Reserve
Makes 4 servings

What a wonderful winter dish and so utterly Canadian, using the highest quality Canadian beef and rich, well-made dark ale. Serve with mounds of lovely mashed potatoes and buttered Brussels sprouts.

1 ¼ cups (300 mL) veal or beef stock
4 strip loin or tenderloin steaks,
    6–8 oz (175 g–225 g) each
¼ tsp (1 mL) cracked black pepper
¼ tsp (1 mL) chopped fresh rosemary
½ tsp (2 mL) canola oil

¼ cup (50 mL) Upper Canada Dark Ale
1 tsp (5 mL) green peppercorns
2 tsp (10 mL) Dijon mustard
1 tsp (5 mL) unsalted butter, cold
½ tsp (2 mL) fine sea salt
¼ tsp (1 mL) ground black pepper

Place the stock in a small saucepan over high heat. Cook until reduced by ½. Set aside.

Season the steaks with cracked pepper and rosemary. Heat a large heavy frying pan over high heat. Once hot, add the oil and beef; sear all steaks on both sides. Remove the steaks from the frying pan and set aside.

Deglaze the pan with the dark ale. Add the reduced stock and green peppercorns, cooking on high heat until the sauce has reduced to ⅓ of its original volume. Remove from the heat and whisk in the mustard and butter. Adjust the seasoning with salt and pepper, if desired.

Preheat the grill to high. Grill the steaks to the desired doneness and top with the warmed sauce.

Grilled Loin of Lamb with Eggplant Caviar

The Charles Inn, Niagara-on-the-Lake
Makes 4 servings
Recommended: Inniskillin Wines Cabernet Franc Reserve

This is the perfect dish for 2 people to prepare, as the lamb should be put on the grill about halfway through cooking the eggplant. Make an effort to find lamb loins; they are often available in frozen form at larger supermarkets or ask a butcher to order them for you.

¼ cup (50 mL) extra virgin olive oil
2 shallots, sliced
2 garlic cloves, thinly sliced
salt to taste

2 medium-sized eggplants, peeled and diced
4 boneless lamb loins

Preheat the grill to medium-high.

In a large pan over medium-high heat, heat the olive oil. Add the shallots and garlic, being careful not to burn the garlic (reduce the heat if necessary). Cook until soft and translucent, about 10 minutes. Add the eggplant and cook until soft, another 5 minutes. Season with salt. Keep warm while grilling the lamb.

Grill the lamb for about 3 minutes on each side, and serve with the eggplant immediately.

Chicken Pot Pie

Kettle Creek Inn, Port Stanley
Recommended: Pelee Island Winery Premium Select Chardonnay
Makes 8 servings

This dish has been on the menu at the Kettle Creek Inn since 1983. It's usually served with a simple salad of fresh greens dressed with a light vinaigrette. What could be better than this classic pie on a blustery winter night?

For the pastry:

1 ¼ cups (300 mL) all-purpose flour

⅓ cup (75 mL) butter, chilled and cubed

½ tsp (2 mL) salt

4–5 Tbsp (60–75 mL) ice water

Combine the flour and salt in a large bowl. Cut in the chilled butter with a pastry cutter. When the mixture resembles coarse meal, sprinkle enough ice water over it to hold the dough together. Press into 2 balls and then flatten each into a disc; wrap with plastic wrap and chill for 30 minutes.

On a floured board, roll out 1 disc to ⅛-inch (0.3 cm) thickness. Place in a 9-inch (27-cm) deep glass pie dish. Trim the edges and refrigerate until ready to fill.

For the chicken filling:

¼ cup (50 mL) butter

1 small onion, diced

1 small leek, white part only, washed, dried and chopped

1 ½ lb (750 g) boneless, skinless chicken breasts, cut into ¾-inch (2-cm) pieces

1 tsp (5 mL) salt

1 tsp (5 mL) ground black pepper

⅔ cup (155 g) white button mushrooms, cleaned and halved

¼ cup (50 mL) all-purpose flour

1 cup (250 mL) dry white wine

1 cup (250 mL) whipping cream

¾ cup (175 mL) whole milk

1 ½ tsp (7 mL) chopped fresh thyme leaves

In a large saucepan over medium heat, melt the butter. Add the onion and leek and cook until translucent, about 5 minutes. Add the chicken, salt and pepper and continue to cook, stirring often, until the chicken is about half-cooked, but not browning. Add the mushrooms and cook for a further 5 minutes. Sprinkle the flour over the mixture and cook for 2–3 minutes (the mixture will be very dry). Add the white wine and simmer until the wine has reduced by ¼. Add the cream, milk and thyme. Reduce the heat and continue to cook until the chicken is fully cooked.

Preheat the oven to 350°F (175°C).

Roll out the remaining pastry disc on a floured surface. Pour the chicken filling into the pastry shell and top with the remaining pastry. Trim and crimp the edges, and cut slits in the top to allow steam to escape. Bake for 25–30 minutes, until the pastry is golden brown on top.

Winter Greens with Duck Confit & Caramelized Pears in Roquefort Dressing

Woodlawn Inn, Cobourg
Recommended: Colio Estate Wines CEV Gamay Noir
Makes 2 servings

Roast the duck legs for this dish ahead of time—even the day before, if you wish. A simple variation on this is to use the meat from a Chinese-style barbecued duck; pick one up from a restaurant on the way home and dinner is almost made.

For the dressing:

1 Tbsp (15 mL) red wine vinegar
½ tsp (2 mL) Pommery mustard
½ tsp (2 mL) granulated sugar
1 oz (30 g) Roquefort cheese

½ cup (125 mL) extra virgin olive oil
salt and freshly ground black pepper
  to taste

In a small mixing bowl, whisk the vinegar, mustard and sugar together. Crumble in the cheese, and gradually whisk in the olive oil in a steady stream. Season with salt and pepper. Set aside.

For the salad:

2 fresh duck legs, 3–4 oz (75–125 g)
  each, skin on
2 garlic cloves, crushed
salt and black pepper to taste
¼ tsp (1 mL) dried rosemary
1 Tbsp (15 mL) extra virgin olive oil

1 Bosc pear, peeled, quartered and
  cored
1 Tbsp (15 mL) granulated sugar
2 cups (500 mL) mixed greens (such as
  escarole, red leaf, Belgian endive)

Preheat the oven to 300°F (150°C).

Rub the duck legs with the garlic; season with salt, pepper and rosemary. Place the duck in a small roasting pan and roast for 1 ½ hours, until the meat is pliable (the duck should be submerged in its own fat while cooking). Remove the duck from the oven and allow to cool slightly. Pull the meat away from the bones and pat dry with paper towel. Set aside.

Heat the olive oil in a small frying pan until very hot, but not smoking. Dust the pear quarters with the granulated sugar and brown on both sides until the pears are a golden caramel colour. Remove from the frying pan and cool slightly. When cool enough to handle, slice each quarter in half.

To serve, toss the duck meat, pears and salad greens in a medium mixing bowl and transfer to serving plates. Drizzle each salad with the Roquefort dressing and serve immediately.

Baked Salmon with Citrus Relish

Ste. Anne's Country Inn & Spa, Grafton
Recommended: Cave Spring Riesling Reserve
Makes 4 servings

The chef at Ste. Anne's uses a dry ginger tea rub on the salmon before baking it and then serves it with a dramatic purple rice pilaf. This variation on that dry rub is based on a green tea, and will be more than you need for four servings; store the remaining dry rub in a jar with a tight-fitting lid. To prepare the rub, you'll need a spice grinder.

For the dry rub:

8 oz (250 g) green tea leaves, ground
¼ cup (50 mL) coarse kosher salt
2 Tbsp (25 mL) black peppercorns,
    cracked

1 tsp (5 mL) ground cardamom
1 Tbsp (15 mL) coriander seeds,
    roasted and ground
1 tsp (5 mL) ground cumin

Place all ingredients in a large resealable plastic bag and shake to combine.

For the salmon:

four 6-oz (170-g) salmon fillets

1 Tbsp (15 mL) olive oil

Coat each salmon fillet with some of the dry rub mixture, rubbing gently onto the skin side of the salmon. Cover with plastic wrap and refrigerate for 1 hour.

Preheat the oven to 375°F (190°C). Grease an ovenproof glass dish with the olive oil and place the salmon rub-side up in the dish. Bake for 15–20 minutes.

For the citrus relish:

2 small limes

1 medium orange

1 large lemon

1 tsp (5 mL) olive oil

1 medium shallot, finely chopped

½ tsp (2.5 mL) salt

½ tsp (2.5 mL) freshly ground black
    pepper

1 Tbsp (15 mL) rice wine vinegar

½ cup (125 mL) apple cider

1 tsp (5 mL) cornstarch

1 Tbsp (15 mL) water

1 tsp (5 mL) chopped cilantro

Zest the rinds of the limes, orange and lemon into a small bowl. Squeeze all of the juice from the fruit and add to the zest; set aside.

Heat the olive oil in a pan over medium heat. Add the shallot, salt and pepper and cook for 1 minute. Deglaze the pan with the rice wine vinegar and reduce until almost completely gone. Add the citrus zest and juice and the apple cider. Cook the mixture until it's reduced by ½.

Mix the cornstarch in a small bowl with the water, and then add the mixture to the pan. Cook for 1 minute. Remove the pan from the heat, add the cilantro and adjust the seasoning to taste. Serve the warm relish with the cooked salmon.

Truffle Shiitake Quinoa Rösti

The Elora Mill Inn, Elora
Recommended: Jackson-Triggs Proprietor's Reserve Pinot Noir
Makes 2 servings

The Elora Mill chef serves these potato and grain rösti with a fricassee of spaghetti squash, asparagus and green kale, topped with creamed leeks. For a simple lunch or light dinner, serve these with scrambled eggs or smoked salmon.

½ cup (125 mL) quinoa
3 large Yukon Gold potatoes, peeled
   and grated
1 cup (250 mL) finely sliced shiitake
   caps
2 Tbsp (25 mL) white truffle oil

1 garlic clove, minced
¼ cup (50 mL) butter, melted
salt and freshly ground black pepper
   to taste
¼ cup (50 mL) canola oil

Combine the quinoa with 1 cup (250 mL) water in a small saucepan and bring to a boil. Reduce to a simmer, cover and cook for 15 minutes, until all the water has been absorbed. Set aside.

Preheat the oven to 400°F (200°C).

Place the grated potatoes in a colander and press with the back of a wooden spoon to drain off some of the excess moisture. Combine the potatoes, shiitakes, truffle oil, garlic, butter, salt and pepper in a large bowl and mix thoroughly.

Heat 2 small ovenproof frying pans on 2 burners over high heat; add 2 Tbsp (25 mL) of canola oil to each frying pan. When the oil is hot, divide the potato mixture evenly between the two frying pans, pressing down on the mixture to flatten it in the pan. Cook for 1 minute, then place the frying pans in the oven and cook for 20 minutes, turning each rösti over at the 10-minute mark. (To flip the rösti, turn it out onto a plate, and slide it back into the pan.) If not serving immediately, reduce the oven temperature to 200°F (95°C) and keep warm until ready to serve.

Thai Black Tiger Shrimps in Red Curry

Eganridge Inn, Country Club & Spa, Fenelon Falls
Recommended: Henry of Pelham Family Estate Off-Dry Riesling
Makes 2 servings

You'll need a food processor to prepare the fabulous curry paste called for in this highly seasoned dish. Or look for a jarred red curry paste at the supermarket or any shops specializing in Asian ingredients. The curry paste may be more than you need for this recipe. Keep any remaining paste refrigerated for up to 3 weeks. Serve the shrimp over basmati rice.

For the red curry paste:

2 medium red bell peppers, seeded and diced

2 lemon grass stalks, finely chopped

2 small onions, diced

8 garlic cloves

2 Tbsp (25 mL) chopped fresh ginger

2 tsp (10 mL) ground coriander seed

2 tsp (10 mL) mustard powder

2 tsp (10 mL) salt

1 tsp (5 mL) ground cinnamon

1 Tbsp (15 mL) brown sugar

2 Tbsp (25 mL) vegetable oil

½ tsp (2 mL) cayenne pepper

Place all the ingredients in a food processor fitted with a metal blade and purée until smooth, using the on/off button. Turn the motor off and scrape down the sides once or twice during processing. Set aside.

For the shrimp:

12 black tiger shrimp, rinsed and shelled

2 Tbsp (25 mL) vegetable oil

⅓ cup (75 mL) unsweetened coconut milk

In a large frying pan over high heat, sauté the shrimp in the oil for 2 minutes, shaking the pan to evenly cook the shrimp. Add ⅓ cup (75 mL) red curry paste and the coconut milk. Simmer for a few minutes and serve immediately.

Caraway-Crusted Rack of Lamb with Cabernet Jus

The Little Inn of Bayfield, Bayfield
Recommended: Inniskillin Wines Klose Vineyard Cabernet Sauvignon
Makes 2 servings

The chef at Little Inn of Bayfield usually serves this dish with Jerusalem artichokes, but suggests that green beans also work well.

For the lamb:

8-rib rack of lamb, trimmed and
frenched

2 Tbsp (25 mL) caraway seeds,
crushed

1 Tbsp (15 mL) coarse sea salt

1 Tbsp (15 mL) coarsely ground black
pepper

1 Tbsp (15 mL) vegetable oil

Preheat the oven to 400°F (200°C). Wrap the exposed lamb bones with foil. Set aside.

In a small bowl mix the crushed caraway seeds, salt and pepper. Spread the spice mixture over the top of the rack, packing the mixture down lightly with your hands.

In a medium-sized heavy frying pan, heat the oil over high heat. Place the lamb in the pan, spice-side up, and sear. Do not sear the lamb on both sides, as the caraway seeds will burn. Place the lamb on a lightly greased baking sheet and bake for 15 minutes. Remove the foil from the bones and bake for a further 20 minutes. Remove the lamb from the oven and let rest for 15 minutes. Meanwhile, prepare the cabernet jus.

For the jus:

1 shallot, finely chopped

1 cup (250 mL) Cabernet Sauvignon

2 cups (500 mL) lamb or chicken stock

2 Tbsp (25 mL) chopped fresh parsley

1 garlic clove, minced

In the same pan used to sear the lamb, sauté the shallot over medium-high heat for a few minutes, until translucent. Add the wine and stock and cook until the jus is reduced by ⅓. Add the parsley and garlic and cook for 1 more minute. Serve immediately with the rack of lamb.

Huron County Five Bean Cassoulet with Black Angus Beef Cheeks

The Little Inn of Bayfield, Bayfield
Recommended: Colio Estate Wines CE Cabernet Merlot
Makes 6 servings

Read this recipe through carefully before beginning and be sure to leave yourself plenty of time, as all the beans need to be soaked for 8 hours (or overnight). A good butcher should be able to obtain beef cheeks for you; if not, substitute large pieces of stewing or braising steak or any cut suitable for slow-cooking.

½ cup (120 mL) pinto beans
½ cup (120 mL) white beans
½ cup (120 mL) black beans
½ cup (120 mL) dark red beans
½ cup (120 mL) Romano beans
4 large beef cheeks, silver skin left on
½ tsp (5 mL) salt
¼ tsp (2 mL) freshly ground black pepper
2 Tbsp (25 mL) all-purpose flour
¼ cup (50 mL) olive oil
2 cups (500 mL) diced carrot
2 cups (500 mL) diced onion

2 cups (500 mL) diced leeks (white part only)
12 garlic cloves (1 head), smashed
4 fresh thyme sprigs
4 fresh bay leaves (or 2 dried)
4 fresh rosemary branches
1 Tbsp (15 mL) peppercorns, crushed
2 cups (475 mL) Merlot
10 cups (2.4 L) veal or beef stock
2 Tbsp (25 mL) cold butter
¼ cup (50 mL) chopped parsley
1 garlic clove, minced

Soak the beans in water overnight. (Use approximately 4 cups/1L water for each ½ cup/125 mL dry beans.) When ready to use the hydrated beans, discard the soaking water and rinse beans thoroughly. Set aside.

Preheat the oven to 350°F (175°C).

Season the beef cheeks with the salt and pepper and then lightly dust them with flour. Heat the olive oil in a large, ovenproof heavy-bottomed pot over medium-high heat. Brown the meat in the hot oil, 3 minutes per side, until golden brown. Remove the meat and reduce the heat to medium. Add the carrot, onion, leek, garlic, thyme, bay leaves, rosemary and crushed peppercorns. Brown the vegetables for 2–3 minutes.

Add the red wine to the pot, scraping all the caramelized residue off the bottom. Return the beef to the pot; add the stock and beans and stir to combine, ensuring everything is fully covered in liquid. Bring to a boil, then reduce the heat to a simmer and adjust the seasoning if necessary. Place the lid on the pot and braise in the preheated oven for 3 hours, or until the beef cheeks are tender.

Remove the pot from the oven and stir in the butter, parsley and minced garlic. Allow to rest for 20 minutes before serving.

Colio Estate Winery

Colio Estate Wines is located in the Lake Erie North Shore viticultural area, in the town of Harrow. This picturesque winery produces over 200,000 cases a year of VQA and other award-winning wines. With one of the longest growing seasons in the country, the North Shore area is blessed with exceptional soil and a micro-climate that is moderated by both the lake and the prevailing southwest winds. Colio Winery is known for its red wines, most notably Cabernet Franc and Merlot. Winemaker Carlo Negri is the recent recipient of the Tony Aspler "Cuvée Award of Excellence," as well as the Ontario Wine Awards "Winemaker of the Year."

Beef in Baco Noir with Porcini & Polenta

Harbour House, Niagara-on-the-Lake
Recommended: Henry of Pelham Family Estate Baco Noir Reserve
Makes 6 servings

This was the main course we created for the Henry of Pelham Wine Maker's Dinner at the Harbour House Hotel alongside their 1998 Baco Noir Reserve. Serve this with the same wine with which it's made. This dish is even better when prepared a day ahead. Serve with crusty bread.

⅓ cup (75 mL) olive oil
3 lb (1.5 kg) stewing beef, excess
    fat trimmed and cut into 1-inch
    (2.5-cm) pieces
1 large onion, chopped
2 good-sized beef marrow bones
4 bay leaves, preferably fresh, or
    2 dried
2 whole cloves

salt and freshly ground black pepper
    to taste
2 cups (500 mL) Henry of Pelham Baco
    Noir
1 Tbsp (15 mL) tomato paste
1 oz (25 g) dried porcini, soaked for
    15 minutes and then strained
    (reserve soaking liquid)
2 ½ cups (625 mL) beef stock

Warm the oil in a Dutch oven or heatproof casserole over medium-high heat. Brown the beef on all sides in two batches. Remove the beef and set aside. Add the onion and sauté for 5 minutes or so, until softened. Return the beef to the pan and add the marrow bones, bay leaves, cloves and a good grinding of salt and pepper. Continue to cook and stir for another 10 minutes, turning the meat and bones over frequently. Splash in the red wine, increase the heat to high and cook for about 10 minutes, until the wine has reduced slightly and the mixture has thickened. Reduce the heat.

Blend the tomato paste into the porcini soaking liquid and add it and the porcini to the meat. Pour in ½ the beef stock, increase the heat and bring to a gentle boil. Reduce the heat to a simmer, cover loosely and cook slowly for about 2 hours, checking occasionally and adding additional stock during the cooking time. Cook until the sauce is nicely thickened and the meat is tender. Use a small spoon to remove the marrow from the bones and add it to the sauce. Discard the bones and bay leaves and serve immediately.

Henry of Pelham

Just like the people responsible for their production, the wines from this premium estate winery on the Niagara Bench are well respected, award-winning and very popular. The Speck brothers—Paul, Matthew and Daniel—have been involved in the world of wine since 1988. The 150 acres of the winery and vineyards were originally deeded to their great great-grandfather in 1794. With the help of winemaker Ron Geisbrecht, the Speck family produces some of the finest wines in the region and country. Their efforts focus on Chardonnay, Riesling, Cabernet Sauvignon, Baco Noir, Pinot Noir, Sauvignon Blanc and Riesling icewine. Vineland and winery tours are offered daily from late May through October. Featuring the best in local produce, the winery's Coach House Cafe offers exceptional Canadian artisanal cheeses and creative food stylings.

Traditional French-Canadian Tourtière

The Vintage Goose Inn & Spa, Kingsville
Recommended: Pelee Island Winery Shiraz Cabernet
Makes 6–8 servings

Serve this rich meat pie with an apple or red onion chutney, and a green salad.

For the filling:

1 lb (500 g) ground pork	1 ½ tsp (7 mL) salt
1 lb (500 g) ground veal	¼ tsp (1 mL) ground cloves
1 medium onion, chopped	½ tsp (2 mL) freshly grated nutmeg
1 large garlic clove, finely chopped	1 cup (250 mL) water
1 tsp (5 mL) freshly ground black pepper	1 slice white bread, cubed

In a large saucepan, combine the pork and veal with the onion, garlic, pepper, salt, cloves, nutmeg and water. Bring to a gentle boil, stirring to blend all the ingredients, then reduce the heat to a simmer. Cook for 20 minutes. Remove from the heat and stir in the bread cubes. Adjust the seasoning. Set aside.

For the pastry:

1 ½ cups (375 mL) all-purpose flour

½ tsp (5 mL) salt

½ cup (125 mL) shortening or lard

3–4 Tbsp (45–60 mL) ice water

milk for brushing

In a mixing bowl combine the flour and salt. Cut in the shortening or lard with a fork or pastry blender until the mixture begins to look crumbly. Stir in the ice water, a little at a time, until you can gather the pastry in a ball in your hands. Wrap the pastry in plastic wrap and allow it to rest in the refrigerator for ½ hour.

Preheat the oven to 400°F (200°C).

On a floured board, roll ⅔ of the pastry to fit a 9-inch (23-cm) pie plate. Pour the meat mixture into the pastry shell and spread it out evenly. Roll out the remaining pastry and use it to cover the top. Pinch the edges of the pastry together and trim. Cut slits in the top to allow steam to escape and brush with a little milk to help it brown. Bake for 45–55 minutes. Allow to rest for 15 minutes. Serve warm.

Tagliatelle al Fungi

The Millcroft Inn & Spa, Alton
Recommended: Inniskillin Founder's Reserve Pinot Noir
Makes 2 main course servings, or 4 appetizer portions

Tagliatelle is the name used in northern Italy for fettuccine. Made with vegetable stock, this is one of the Millcroft's all-time favourites in late winter and early spring. Use fresh pasta for this recipe.

3 Tbsp (45 mL) olive oil
¼ cup (50 mL) shiitake mushrooms, cleaned and sliced
¼ cup (50 mL) button mushrooms, cleaned and sliced
¼ cup (50 mL) morel mushrooms, cleaned and sliced
1 cup (250 mL) portobello mushrooms, cleaned and diced
salt and freshly ground black pepper to taste
1 shallot, diced

2 garlic cloves, chopped
1 cup (250 mL) dry white wine
1 cup (250 mL) chicken stock
1 lb (500 g) fresh tagliatelle
10 basil leaves, washed, dried and shredded
¼ cup (50 mL) chopped Italian parsley
⅓ cup (75 mL) butter, cubed
2 tsp (10 mL) truffle oil
¼ cup (50 mL) grated Parmigiano-Reggiano

In a large frying pan, heat the olive oil over high heat. Add all the mushrooms, salt and pepper and sauté for 5 minutes. Add the shallot and garlic and sauté for 1 minute further. Add the white wine and cook until it's reduced by ½. Add the chicken stock and reduce again by ½.

Add the pasta to a pot of boiling water and cook while you finish the mushroom sauce.

Add the basil, parsley, butter and truffle oil to the mushrooms. Drain the cooked pasta and add to the frying pan, shaking the pan gently to coat the pasta.

Garnish with the cheese and a drizzle of olive oil, if desired.

Duck Breast in Maple Syrup & Lime Glaze

The Inn at Manitou, McKellar
Recommended: Inniskillin Wines Pinot Noir Reserve
Makes 4 servings

A perfect entrée for entertaining. Serve this dish on a bed of cooked baby rapini.

2 skinless, boneless duck breasts
½ cup (125 mL) maple syrup
1 lime, sliced
salt and freshly ground black pepper
    to taste

juice of 2 limes
2 ½ cups (625 mL) chicken stock
2 Tbsp (25 mL) butter

Place the duck breasts in a plastic container. Cover with the maple syrup, sliced lime, salt and pepper; cover and refrigerate for 1 hour.

Preheat the oven to 450°F (230°C).

Remove the duck from the marinade, discarding the lime slices but reserving the rest of the marinade. Place the duck in a small roasting pan, and brush with some of the reserved marinade. Roast for 8–10 minutes. Remove the duck from the oven and let it rest for at least 5 minutes.

While the duck breasts are cooking, heat the marinade in a medium-sized, heavy pot over medium-high heat. When the mixture turns a golden colour, add the lime juice and chicken stock. Bring to a gentle boil and reduce by ½. Remove the pan from the heat and whisk in the butter. Keep warm until ready to use.

To serve, slice breasts, pour sauce over duck and serve immediately.

Pork Tenderloin with Mushrooms Inside & Out

HighFields Country Inn & Spa, Zephyr
Recommended: Cave Spring Cellars Pinot Noir
Makes 6–8 servings

In this whimsically named dish, the pork is stuffed with a mushroom filling and then rolled in a dry mushroom powder, both of which help to keep the meat moist and flavourful. Use any assortment of mushrooms you like.

For the filling:
2 Tbsp (25 mL) butter
1 cup (250 mL) sliced button
   mushrooms
1 cup (250 mL) sliced shiitake
   mushrooms

1 small onion, diced
1 large garlic clove, minced
1 tsp (5 mL) dried thyme
¼ cup (50 mL) tomato juice

In a large pan over medium-high heat, melt the butter and sauté the mushrooms and onion together for 10 minutes, until almost all the liquid has evaporated. Add the garlic, thyme and tomato juice. Cook until most of the liquid has evaporated once more. You should have about 1 ½ cups (375 mL) of filling. Set aside to cool.

For the tenderloin:
2 pork tenderloin, 12–14 oz
   (375–425 g), trimmed of fat and
   silver skin
salt and freshly ground black pepper
   to taste ½ cup (125 mL) crushed
   dried mushrooms

1 Tbsp (15 mL) vegetable oil
½ cup (125 mL) dry white wine
½ cup (125 mL) chicken stock
1 Tbsp (15 mL) truffle oil

Make an incision in each tenderloin to form a pocket, making sure not to cut the meat from end to end, or all the way through. Fill each pocket with ⅔ cup (150 mL) of the mushroom filling, pressing it well into the pocket. Sprinkle the tenderloins with salt and pepper and set aside.

Place the crushed dried mushrooms in a food processor, blender or spice grinder and grind until fine. Transfer the mushroom powder to a large plate and roll both tenderloins in the powder.

Preheat the oven to 350°F (175°C).

Heat the vegetable oil in a large ovenproof frying pan over high heat. Sauté the tenderloins until brown on all sides. Place in the oven and roast for 10 minutes. When done, remove to a cutting board to rest.

Deglaze the frying pan with the white wine and chicken stock. Bring the mixture to a boil, then reduce the heat to simmer. Adjust the seasoning to taste and add the truffle oil. Remove the sauce from the heat.

To serve, slice the tenderloins and spoon the sauce over top.

Sweets for All Seasons

Fruit-filled tarts, luscious tortes and cakes, superlative chocolate sweets, spiced muffins, creamy parfaits, sticky puddings, chunky cookies sandwiched with ice cream, fragrant fruit cobblers and old-fashioned crisps —all of these and much more head up the dessert menu at Ontario's Finest Inns. For many, dessert is the most anticipated course, and the pastry and dessert chefs at the inns don't disappoint. How sweet that is.

Chapter Seven

SWEETS FOR ALL SEASONS

Roasted Pineapple with Rum Caramel

Sam Jakes Inn, Merrickville
Makes 4 servings

At the Sam Jakes Inn, the caramel sauce for the pineapple is accentuated with a little chile and whole peppercorns—simply add 1 small jalapeño, seeded and finely chopped, and a few black peppercorns to the ingredient list for the caramel sauce. Serve with good-quality vanilla ice cream or frozen yogurt.

2 ripe pineapples, peeled, cored and
    cut into 8 wedges
2 cups (500 mL) light brown sugar
⅓ cup (75 mL) rum
¼ cup (50 mL) lemon juice
2 Tbsp (25 mL) minced fresh ginger

1 ¼ cups (300 mL) water
⅓ cup (75 mL) butter, chilled and cut
    into pieces
1 vanilla bean, split lengthwise
2 bananas, peeled, sliced in ½-inch
    (1 cm) rounds

Place the pineapple in a greased baking dish in a single layer. Set aside.

Combine the brown sugar, rum, lemon juice, ginger and water in a medium-sized, heavy saucepan over low heat. Stir constantly until the sugar melts and completely dissolves. Increase the heat to medium and bring the mixture to a boil, then reduce to a simmer and cook for about 30 seconds. Whisk in the butter, piece by piece, whisking well after each addition. After the last piece of butter has been added, continue whisking for another 30 seconds. Scrape the vanilla beans from the pod into the mixture and stir well. Remove the saucepan from the heat. Preheat the oven to 275°F (140°C).

Return the caramel sauce to a low heat and carefully add the banana. Stir gently with a wooden spoon.

Pour the caramel sauce over the pineapple wedges and bake for about 1 hour, basting every 10 minutes. When the pineapple looks translucent, remove from the oven and serve.

Warm Molten Chocolate Cake
with Crème Anglaise

Merrill Inn, Picton
Makes 8 servings

At the Merrill Inn, this cake is served with a pistachio crème anglaise. You can achieve this by simply adding 1 Tbsp (15 mL) pistachio paste to the crème anglaise recipe below, or sprinkle a few chopped unsalted pistachios over the cakes before serving. Pistachio paste is available from fine food shops and those that specialize in unusual ingredients for baking. You'll need eight 4-oz (125-g) custard cups for this recipe.

For the crème anglaise:

3 egg yolks	½ cup (125 mL) milk
4 Tbsp (60 mL) granulated sugar	½ cup (125 mL) heavy cream

In a medium-sized, heavy pot, whisk together the egg yolks and 2 Tbsp (25 mL) of the sugar. Set aside.

Place the milk, cream and remaining sugar in a small saucepan. Add the pistachio paste, if desired. Bring to a boil and remove from the heat.

Slowly pour the hot cream mixture over the yolk and sugar mixture, whisking constantly to avoid cooking the eggs. When combined, place over medium heat, stirring constantly until the mixture just coats the back of a wooden spoon.

Strain through a fine sieve into a small bowl and cover with plastic wrap. Press the wrap to the surface, to prevent a skin from forming. Set aside to cool to room temperature.

For the cakes:

2 Tbsp (25 mL) butter, softened

¼ cup (50 mL) granulated sugar

4 ½ oz (140 g) bittersweet chocolate,
    cut into small pieces

¼ cup (50 mL) butter

3 eggs, at room temperature

3 egg yolks, at room temperature

1 ½ Tbsp (22 mL) granulated sugar

1 Tbsp (15 mL) all-purpose flour

⅓ cup (75 mL) unsalted pistachios,
    roughly chopped (optional)

Grease 8 custard cups with the softened butter and coat with the ¼ cup (50 mL) sugar. Set aside.

Melt the chocolate and the ¼ cup (50 mL) butter in a double boiler. Combine thoroughly, then transfer to a large mixing bowl and keep warm.

Combine the eggs, yolks, and 1 ½ Tbsp (22 mL) sugar in a medium-sized bowl. Using the whisk attachment of an electric mixer, beat on high speed for 10 minutes, until thick and fluffy. Fold ¼ of the melted chocolate into the egg mixture, then pour it over the remaining melted chocolate in the large bowl. Gently fold together while sprinkling in the flour. Work quickly so the mixture retains as much air as possible.

Ladle the batter into the prepared cups until filled to ½ inch (1 cm) below the rim. Refrigerate until cold.

Preheat the oven to 350°F (180°C).

Arrange the custard cups on a baking sheet and bake for 8–10 minutes—no longer, as the cakes should be soft and runny on the inside. Let stand for 10 minutes.

Carefully pull the cake away from the sides of the cups by gently tilting the cups. Invert the cakes onto serving plates and drizzle the crème anglaise around the cake. Top with pistachios, if using.

Espresso Milk Chocolate Mousse & Almond Cookie Sandwiches

The Westover Inn, St. Marys
Makes 4–6 servings

This elegant dessert might seem complicated, but the components may be made ahead of time and assembled just before serving. Vary this recipe by substituting walnuts or pecans for the almonds and vanilla extract for the almond extract.

For the mousse:

½ envelope unflavoured gelatin powder

¼ cup (50 mL) whipping cream

1 ¼ tsp (6 mL) butter

1 Tbsp (15 mL) instant espresso granules

6 oz (175 g) milk chocolate, chopped

1 cup (250 mL) whipping cream

Soften the gelatin according to package directions; set aside.

Combine the ¼ cup (50 mL) whipping cream, butter and espresso in a small saucepan over medium heat. When the coffee granules have dissolved, remove from the heat.

Place the chopped chocolate in a double boiler. Once the chocolate has begun to melt, add the coffee mixture and stir until the chocolate has melted. Add the gelatin and blend well. Transfer to a large mixing bowl and let cool.

Whip the 1 cup (250 mL) whipping cream in a separate bowl until soft peaks form. Fold approximately ½ of the whipped cream into the chocolate mixture. Carefully fold in the remaining whipped cream. Cover and refrigerate.

For the cookies:

1 cup (250 mL) bread flour

¼ tsp (1 mL) baking soda

¼ tsp (1 mL) baking powder

1 cup (250 mL) butter

1 ½ cups (375 mL) granulated sugar

1 tsp (5 mL) almond extract

½ cup (125 mL) almonds, toasted and finely ground

Sift the flour, baking soda and baking powder together. Set aside.

In a large mixing bowl, cream together the butter, sugar and almond extract until light and fluffy. Mix in the dry ingredients. Stir in the ground almonds. Transfer the dough to a sheet of plastic wrap and wrap tightly. Chill until firm.

Preheat the oven to 350°F (180°C). Lightly grease 2 baking sheets.

Sprinkle some flour on a clean surface and roll out the cookie dough to a ⅛-inch (.3-cm) thickness. Use a 3-inch (7.5-cm) round cookie cutter to cut shapes out of the dough. Transfer to the prepared baking sheets.

Bake for 5–8 minutes, until the cookies are just light brown around the edges. Let cool on a wire rack.

To assemble, place a small scoop of chocolate mousse between 2 cooled cookies.

Peach-Raspberry Upside-Down Cake

Kettle Creek Inn, Port Stanely
Recommended: Pelee Island Winery Cabernet Franc Icewine
Makes 8–10 servings

A lovely variation on a very popular theme. Serve this cake just this side of warm or at room temperature with fresh whipped cream, peach ice cream or a raspberry sorbet.

For the fruit:

¼ cup (50 mL) butter
¾ cup (175 mL) packed brown sugar
½ cup (125 mL) hazelnuts, toasted and chopped

8 fresh peaches, peeled, pitted, halved
1 cup (250 mL) fresh raspberries

Melt the butter and pour into a 9-inch (1.5 L) cake pan. Sprinkle the sugar and hazelnuts evenly over the butter. Arrange the peaches, cut side down, over the sugar and nuts. Sprinkle the raspberries over the peaches.

For the batter:

½ cup (125 mL) butter, softened
¾ cup (175 mL) granulated sugar
2 eggs, at room temperature
1 ½ tsp (6 mL) vanilla extract
1 ½ cups (375 mL) all-purpose flour

1 ½ tsp (6 mL) baking soda
1 tsp (5 mL) baking powder
¼ tsp (1 mL) salt
1 cup (250 mL) sour cream
⅓ cup (75 mL) buttermilk

Preheat the oven to 350°F (180°C).

In a large bowl, cream together the butter and sugar. Beat in the eggs one at a time. Add the vanilla.

Mix the flour, baking soda, baking powder and salt in a small bowl. Blend the sour cream and buttermilk in a small bowl. Add the flour mixture to the egg and sugar mixture and mix until combined. Add the sour cream mixture and mix well with a whisk. Pour the batter over the prepared peaches in the cake pan, distributing it evenly. Give the pan a sharp rap on the counter.

Bake for 50–60 minutes, or until a tester inserted in the centre comes out clean. Cool to room temperature (or a little warmer) on a wire rack.

When ready to serve, carefully invert the cake on a serving platter. If any of the topping remains in the pan, simply replace it on the surface of the cake.

Caramelized Apple & Nut Tarts

The Westover Inn, St. Marys
Recommended: Henry of Pelham Family Estate Late Harvest Vidal
Makes 6 servings

These tarts are usually served at the Westover Inn with roasted pear sorbet.
They're also very good with whipped cream or good-quality vanilla ice cream.
Look for the tart shells in the supermarket freezer.

six 3-inch (7.5-cm) sweetened tart shells
⅔ cup (150 mL) mixed unsalted nuts, coarsely chopped
4 Golden Delicious apples, peeled, cored, halved and cubed
⅓ cup (75 mL) butter
¾ cup (175 mL) granulated sugar

Preheat the oven to 325°F (160°C).

Place the tart shells in their foil cups on a baking tray. Place 2 Tbsp (25 mL) of mixed nuts in each shell. Bake in the oven for approximately 10 minutes or until the shells and nuts are a light brown, watching them carefully as nuts can burn easily. Remove the tarts from the oven and allow to cool on a baking rack. When the tarts are completely cooled, carefully take them out of the foil cups and return them to the baking tray.

In a large heavy saucepan, melt the butter over high heat. Sprinkle the sugar over the butter but do not stir. Immediately place the apple pieces in the pan, spreading them evenly over the entire surface—again, do not stir. Allow the apples to cook for 10 minutes. Reduce the heat to medium-high and gently stir. Turn the apples over and allow them to cook for a further 20 minutes, stirring gently once every 5 minutes.

Preheat the oven to 350°F (180°C).

After 30 minutes of cooking time in total, remove the apples from the heat and spoon the filling into the prepared tart shells. Bake for 10 minutes, until golden brown. Cool on a baking rack before serving.

Fresh Mixed Berries in a Phyllo Cup

Ste. Anne's Country Inn & Spa, Grafton
Recommended: Henry of Pelham Family Estate Cabernet Franc Icewine
Makes 4 servings

Delightfully easy to make, this spa-inspired dessert is the perfect choice during berry season. Vary the berries according to availability.

For the phyllo cups:

4 sheets phyllo pastry

1 Tbsp (15 mL) grape seed oil

For the berries:

1 cup (250 mL) plain yogurt

1 tsp (5 mL) liquid honey

½ medium pink grapefruit, zest and juice

2 sprigs fresh mint

pinch ground cardamom

½ cup (125 mL) fresh blueberries

½ cup (125 mL) fresh raspberries

1 cup (250 mL) fresh strawberries, sliced

Drain yogurt overnight in a strainer lined with cheesecloth.

Preheat oven to 350°F (180°C). Place sheets of phyllo pastry on a work surface. Brush half of each pastry sheet with grape seed oil. Fold each sheet in half and cut each into three strips. Place three strips in a muffin tin to form a cup with edges pointing up. Repeat for each remaining cup. Bake 6–8 minutes until golden brown.

Take four small pieces of the mint sprigs and set aside for garnish. Finely chop the rest of the sprigs.

Fold the grapefruit juice and zest, cardamom, honey and chopped mint into the yogurt cheese. Spoon the yogurt cheese into the bottom of the phyllo cups. Top with the berries and garnish with a mint sprig.

Brandied Plum Crêpes

The Westover Inn, St. Marys
Makes approximately 25 crêpes

This recipe may seem daunting until you realize you can easily make the crêpes ahead of time and even freeze them until they're needed. Before cooking them, prepare squares of parchment or wax paper to separate each finished crêpe.

For the brandied plum sauce:

7 large plums, washed and pitted
2 Tbsp (25 mL) brandy
½ cup (125 mL) water
½ cup (125 mL) plum jelly
¼ cup (50 mL) brown sugar, packed

Cut the plums into ½-inch (1.2-cm) pieces. Mix all the ingredients in a large saucepan. Cook over medium heat, stirring occasionally, until the plums are soft and coated in syrup. Remove from the heat and let cool before using.

For the crêpes:

4 eggs
2 cups (500 mL) milk
1 tsp (5 mL) brandy
¼ cup (50 mL) butter, melted and
cooled to room temperature
1 tsp (5 mL) salt
2 cups (500 mL) all-purpose flour
¼ cup (50 mL) brown sugar, packed

In a medium-sized bowl whisk the eggs until well blended. In a large measuring cup, combine the milk, brandy and butter. Add the milk mixture to the eggs and whisk well until combined.

Combine the salt, flour and sugar in a large bowl and stir well. Add the wet ingredients to the dry mixture all at once and mix well. Set the batter aside to rest for 20 minutes before using.

Heat a small non-stick pan over medium-high heat. Using a small ladle, pour a portion of the batter into the hot pan and swirl the batter around to coat the entire bottom of the pan. Cook for approximately 30 seconds, loosen the edges with a metal spatula and then flip the crêpe to cook for a further 20 seconds on the other side. Remove to parchment or wax paper and repeat with the remaining batter.

To serve, place a small scoop of plum sauce in the centre of each crêpe and fold in ½.

If not serving immediately, the crêpes can be reheated in a 300°F (150°C) oven for 5–10 minutes before filling with plum sauce.

Sticky Toffee Pudding

The Merrill Inn, Picton
Recommended: Inniskillin Wines Late Harvest Vidal
Makes 6 individual puddings

You will need six 1-cup (250-mL) cake molds for this recipe, a classic English preparation that is especially good during the cold weather. Serve with softly whipped cream or pouring cream.

¼ cup (50 mL) chopped dried apricots
¼ cup (50 mL) chopped dried cranberries
¼ cup (50 mL) chopped dried figs
¼ cup (50 mL) chopped pitted dates
1 cup (250 mL) water
1 tsp (5 mL) baking soda
¼ cup (50 mL) unsweetened applesauce, strained
¾ cup (175 mL) all-purpose flour
1 tsp (5 mL) ground cinnamon

½ tsp (2 mL) baking powder
¼ tsp (1 mL) ground allspice
pinch nutmeg
pinch salt
⅓ cup (75 mL) unsalted butter, softened
½ cup (125 mL) brown sugar
2 large eggs, at room temperature
1 tsp (5 mL) grated lemon zest
½ tsp (2 mL) almond extract

Preheat the oven to 350°F (180°C). Lightly grease six 1-cup (250-mL) cake molds and place the molds on a baking sheet. Set aside.

Combine the dried apricots, cranberries, figs, dates and water in a small saucepan and bring to a boil. Reduce the heat and simmer until all the liquid has evaporated. Remove the pan from the heat, stir in the baking soda and cool. When the mixture is at room temperature, mix in the applesauce. Set aside.

Sift together the flour, cinnamon, baking powder, allspice, nutmeg and salt. Set aside.

In a large bowl, cream the butter and brown sugar until light and fluffy. Add the eggs one at a time, beating well after each addition. Beat in the lemon zest and almond extract. Add the dried fruit mixture and flour mixture alternately to the butter and sugar, mixing until just combined.

Spoon the batter into the prepared molds and place the baking sheet on the centre rack of the oven. Bake the puddings for 20–30 minutes, or until a tester comes out clean.

Let the puddings cool slightly, then turn out onto serving plates. Serve while still warm.

Quince Preserves

The Little Inn of Bayfield, Bayfield
Makes approximately 2½ cups (625 mL)

Believe it or not, fragrant quince grow in abundance in the region of Bayfield. Because quince have a high pectin content—and, by the way, taste much better cooked than raw—they are perfect candidates for jams, jellies, preserves and chutneys. This particular preserve is also used to make quince ice cream, and is served with biscotti at the pretty Little Inn of Bayfield.

1 lb (500 g) quince, washed and scrubbed, removing all fuzz	1 cup (250 mL) water
	1 cup (250 mL) Calvados
1½ cups (375 mL) granulated sugar	zest and juice of 1 large lemon

Combine all ingredients in a medium-large heavy pot. Cook over low heat, stirring frequently with a wooden spoon, for about 2 hours, or until you have a soft pulp. Cool, and then process through a food mill.

Fill small, sterilized jars with the preserve and refrigerate. The preserves will keep for about 3 weeks.

Chilled Wild Berry Yogurt Dessert Soup

The Hillcrest, A Valenova Inn & Spa, Port Hope
Makes 4 servings

Whether you tag it a dessert soup or a smoothie, this beautifully coloured concoction is perfect at breakfast or brunch. The Hillcrest uses wild berries, but cultivated berries will do just fine. Make sure the berries are quite ripe, which will enhance the flavour immeasurably. Serve in glasses at breakfast or brunch, or in glass dishes if you wish to serve it as a dessert. It can also be frozen in ice cube trays and reblended to create a refreshing slushy.

1 cup (250 mL) good-quality plain
    yogurt
1 cup (250 mL) freshly squeezed
    orange juice
½ cup (125 mL) pure maple syrup
½ cup (125 mL) spring water

2½ cups (625 mL) assorted fresh
    berries (strawberries, blueberries,
    raspberries, blackberries)
mint sprigs, washed and dried for
    garnish (optional)

Place all the ingredients except the mint in an upright blender and liquefy until smooth. If the mixture seems too thick, add a little more orange juice. Garnish with fresh mint, if using.

Upside-Down Cranberry-Apple Coffee Cake

Harbour House, Niagara-on the-Lake
Recommended: Cave Spring Cellars Indian Summer Riesling
Makes 8 servings

The Harbour House has several preparations, like this one, that are especially designed to be enjoyed at breakfast or any time you need something sweet with coffee or tea.

For the cranberry-apple topping:

1 cup (250 mL) fresh or frozen cranberries, thawed

1 cup (250 mL) finely chopped unpeeled apples

½ cup (125 mL) granulated sugar

½ cup (175 mL) walnuts or almonds, roughly chopped

½ tsp (2 mL) ground cinnamon

¼ tsp (1 mL) ground cloves

Preheat the oven to 350°F (180°C). Grease an 8-inch (1.2 L) round cake pan. Combine all the ingredients in a medium-sized mixing bowl. Spoon the mixture into the prepared pan and set aside.

For the cake:

1 cup (250 mL) all-purpose flour

1 cup (250 mL) granulated sugar

¼ cup (50 mL) butter, melted

¼ cup (50 mL) vegetable oil

2 large eggs, at room temperature

1 tsp (5 mL) pure vanilla extract

Combine all the ingredients in a large mixing bowl and beat at medium speed with an electric mixer for 2 minutes. Spoon the batter over the cranberry mixture.

Bake for 45 minutes or until a tester inserted in the centre comes out clean. Cool for 5 minutes and invert onto a serving platter. Serve warm or at room temperature.

Iced Whisky Parfait with Cranachan

The Breadalbane Inn, Fergus
Makes 10–12 servings

It's fitting that an inn with such a strong Scottish pedigree should feature this variation on a traditional Scottish dish. Often a favourite choice for Burns Night suppers, this dessert can easily be halved to make 6 servings. If you're pressed for time, the parfaits don't have to be frozen. Be sure, though, to keep them refrigerated until serving. Be vigilant when toasting the oatmeal so that it doesn't brown too quickly or too much.

1 cup (250 mL) rolled oats	2 cups (500 mL) whipping cream
1 cup (250 mL) whipping cream	1 ½ cups (375 mL) granulated sugar
⅓ cup (75 mL) whisky	8 large egg yolks

Preheat the oven to 350°F (180°C). Spread the rolled oats on a non-stick baking sheet and toast until golden brown, about 8–10 minutes. Set aside to cool.

In a small saucepan, heat the 1 cup (250 mL) whipping cream and whisky gently over low heat. Cool slightly.

In a mixing bowl, whip the 2 cups (500 mL) whipping cream until medium-stiff peaks form. Set aside.

Beat the sugar and egg yolks in a large bowl with a whisk until pale in colour. Slowly add the cream and whisky mixture, whisking constantly to make sure the eggs don't cook. Fold in the whipped cream in two stages, to ensure that the parfait remains light. Gently fold in the toasted oats.

Spoon the parfait into serving glasses and freeze until firm, about 3–4 hours. About 20 minutes before serving, remove the parfaits from the freezer.

Lemon Tart

The Little Inn of Bayfield, Bayfield
Makes one 10-inch (25-cm) tart, approximately 8 servings

Serve this wonderful tart on its own or with a dollop of barely sweet whipped cream. Make sure to leave enough time for the tart to set.

For the pastry:

1 cup (250 mL) unsalted butter, at room temperature
⅓ cup (75 mL) granulated sugar
4 egg yolks

finely grated zest of 1 lemon
2 cups (500 mL) pastry flour
1 tsp (5 mL) salt

Cream the butter and sugar together until smooth. Blend in the egg yolks and lemon zest.

Stir in the pastry flour and salt and mix just until the dough comes together. Turn out onto a lightly floured surface and knead very gently for 30 seconds. Shape the dough into a disc, wrap and chill for at least an hour. If making dough far in advance, take the dough from the refrigerator an hour before rolling.

On a lightly floured surface, knead the dough again for 30 seconds. Roll out the pastry to ¼-inch (.6-cm) thickness. Line a 10-inch (25-cm) removable-bottom tart pan with the dough. Trim off the extra pastry and chill for 30 minutes.

Preheat the oven to 375°F (190°C).

Prick the crust bottom with a fork and line the shell with parchment paper and pie weights (dried beans or peas also work). Bake for 10 minutes. Remove the pie weights and parchment and return the shell to the oven for another 10–15 minutes, until the edges are lightly browned and the centre is dry. Set aside to cool while preparing the filling.

For the filling:

2 large eggs, at room temperature
3 large egg yolks, at room temperature
1 cup (250 mL) granulated sugar
¾ cup (175 mL) butter, chilled and cut
    into 8 equal pieces

½ cup (125 mL) freshly squeezed
    lemon juice
grated zest of 2 lemons

In the top of a double boiler set over low-medium heat (the water should just be simmering), combine the eggs, yolks and sugar. Whisk frequently for 8–10 minutes, until the mixture is thick and pale lemon in colour.

Add the butter piece by piece, allowing each to melt before adding the next piece.

Add the lemon juice and zest. Continue to cook, whisking frequently, until the curd is thick and custard-like in consistency and the first bubbles appear on the surface, about 4 minutes. The mixture should not boil.

Pour into the pie shell and smooth with a spatula. Cool to room temperature until set, about 1 hour. Cover the tart loosely with plastic wrap and refrigerate for 2 hours. Allow the tart to return to room temperature before serving.

Eagle Lake Rhubarb Crisp

Sir Sam's Inn & WaterSpa, Haliburton
Makes 4–6 servings

The cardamom in this spring crisp is an inspired bit of alchemy. It elevates the flavours of the rhubarb and makes for a more sophisticated fruit dessert. Serve this with whipped cream or ice cream, if desired.

3 cups (750 mL) rhubarb, cut into
  ½-inch (1.2-cm) pieces
1 cup (250 mL) granulated sugar
¼ cup (50 mL) pastry flour, sifted
½ cup (125 mL) butter, at room
  temperature

½ cup (125 mL) brown sugar, packed
2 tsp (10 mL) ground cardamom
  (optional)
½ cup (125 mL) rolled oats

Preheat the oven to 350°F (180°C). Grease a 9-inch (23-cm) square glass baking dish.

Mix the rhubarb and granulated sugar in a medium-sized mixing bowl. Add the flour and toss to combine. Spread the mixture evenly over the bottom of the prepared baking dish. Set aside.

In a large bowl, cream the butter, brown sugar and cardamom, if using. Add the rolled oats and mix well. Spread this mixture over the rhubarb.

Bake for 40 minutes, or until the rhubarb is tender and the topping is golden brown. Cool for 10 minutes before serving.

Sir Sam's Maple Crème Caramel

Sir Sam's Inn & WaterSpa, Haliburton
Recommended: Pelee Island Winery Late Harvest Vidal
Makes 6 servings

The chef at Sir Sam's sometimes adds 1 cup (250 mL) melted white chocolate to this mixture just before the custard is poured into the ramekins. You'll need six 2- or 3-inch (5- or 7.5-cm) ramekins for this recipe.

¼ cup (50 mL) Ontario maple syrup
6 large egg yolks
½ cup (125 mL) granulated sugar
2 cups (500 mL) whipping cream
2 tsp (10 mL) pure vanilla extract

1 tsp (5 mL) ground cinnamon
(optional)
6 fresh mint sprigs, washed and dried
1 ¼ cups (300 mL) fresh strawberries,
washed and hulled

Preheat the oven to 350°F (180°C).

Divide the maple syrup evenly between the 6 ramekins, making sure to coat the bottoms and all sides. Set aside.

In a large mixing bowl, combine the egg yolks, sugar, cream, vanilla and cinnamon, if using. Distribute evenly between the prepared ramekins.

Place the ramekins in a roasting pan. Add boiling water to the pan until it reaches 1 inch (2.5 cm) up the sides of the ramekins. Bake for approximately 45 minutes, until the custard sets. Remove and chill.

Just before serving, run a hot knife around the inside edge of each ramekin to loosen the custards. Invert onto serving plates and garnish with mint and strawberries.

Orange Chocolate Truffle Tart

The Gananoque Inn, Gananoque
Makes 6 servings

This simple yet elegant chocolate tart may be served on its own or with a dollop of whipped cream. It's easy to pull together thanks to a base of chocolate cookie crumbs.

For the tart bottom:

1 ⅓ cups (325 mL) chocolate cookie crumbs

¼ cup (50 mL) butter, softened

Preheat the oven to 350°F (180°C).

Combine the cookie crumbs and butter until evenly moistened. Pat evenly into the bottom and up the sides of an 8-inch (20-cm) tart pan with a removable base. Bake for about 10 minutes, or until firm. Let cool.

For the filling:

8 oz (250 g) good-quality semi-sweet chocolate (such as Lindt), coarsely chopped

¾ cup (175 mL) whipping cream

zest from 1 large orange (the chef recommends organic, if possible)

Melt the chocolate in a heavy saucepan over low heat, being very careful not to scorch the bottom. (Or use a microwave to melt the chocolate.) Stir in the cream and orange zest, and continue stirring for a few minutes, until the mixture is slightly thickened. Pour the chocolate mixture into the cooled tart shell and chill in the refrigerator until fully set, at least 2 hours.

Bring the tart to room temperature before serving.

White Chocolate & Pecan Cookies

The Waring House Inn, Picton
Makes approximately 2 ½ dozen cookies

These cookies appear weekly on the popular Sunday buffet table at the Waring House Inn. Make sure to toast the pecans first, as this adds a wonderful complexity to the cookies. This dough freezes well, and can be baked as required.

1 cup (250 mL) butter
1 cup (250 mL) brown sugar, packed
1 cup (250 mL) granulated sugar
2 eggs, at room temperature
2 tsp (10 mL) pure vanilla extract
2 ½ cups (625 mL) all-purpose flour

1 tsp (5 mL) baking soda
1 tsp (5 mL) salt
2 cups (500 mL) white chocolate
    chunks or chips
1 cup (250 mL) pecans, toasted, cooled
    and roughly chopped

Preheat the oven to 350°F (180°C). Line 2 or 3 baking sheets with parchment paper.

In a large mixing bowl, cream together the butter and both sugars. Beat with an electric mixer until light and fluffy. Add the eggs one at a time, beating well after each addition. Beat in the vanilla.

In a medium-sized mixing bowl, combine the flour, baking soda and salt, stirring well. Add to the butter mixture gradually, in 2 or 3 stages.

Stir in the chocolate and pecans by hand. Using a 1 ½-inch (4-cm) ice cream scoop, drop the dough onto the prepared baking sheets, leaving room between each scoop for the cookie to spread during baking (each sheet should have no more than 5 scoops of dough).

Bake for 12 minutes, until golden brown. Cool the cookies on the baking sheet for a few minutes, and then transfer carefully to a rack to cool completely.

Hana's Famous Great Canadian Butter Tart

Eganridge Inn, Country Club and Spa, Fenelon Falls
Recommended: Strewn Winery Select Late Harvest Vidal
Makes 24 small tarts, or 12 large tarts

At Eganridge Inn these terrific tarts are made in large, individual tart pans and served warm with the wonderful vanilla ice cream made locally at the Kawartha Dairy. A Canadian classic if ever there was one.

For the pastry:

2 cups (500 mL) all-purpose flour
½ tsp (2 ml) salt
1 tsp (5 mL) baking powder
½ cup (125 mL) butter, chilled and cut
    into ½-inch (1.2-cm) pieces

½ cup (125 mL) lard, cut into ½-inch
    (1.2-cm) pieces
2–4 Tbsp (25–60 mL) ice water

Mix the flour, salt and baking powder in a large bowl. Cut in the butter and lard with a pastry cutter until the mixture resembles coarse meal. Sprinkle 2 Tbsp (25 mL) of the ice water over the mixture and knead the dough very gently by hand, adding more water if necessary, just until the dough holds together. Shape the dough into 2 discs and wrap separately in plastic wrap. Refrigerate for at least an hour.

On a floured surface, roll out the discs of pastry one at a time, to about ⅛-inch (0.3-cm) thickness. Cut rounds to fit tart pans.

Preheat the oven to 375°F (190°C) and prepare the filling.

For the filling:

⅔ cup (150 mL) butter
1 cup (250 mL) corn syrup
1 cup (250 mL) packed brown sugar

2 eggs, beaten
½ cup (125 mL) raisins
½ cup (125 mL) walnuts (optional)

Combine the butter, corn syrup and sugar in a heavy-bottomed saucepan over medium heat. Cook until the butter is melted and the sugar is thoroughly dissolved, about 5 minutes or so. Remove from the heat and allow mixture to cool slightly.

Whisk in the eggs, blending until the mixture becomes glossy.

Sprinkle a few raisins and walnuts (if using) into the tart shells. Fill each tart shell no more than ⅔ full with the filling.

Bake until the tarts are golden brown, 15–20 minutes. Serve at room temperature or slightly warm.

Strewn Winery

Located just outside Niagara-on-the-Lake's Old Town, Strewn Winery enjoys Niagara's "cool climate," which allows many grape varieties to develop to full maturity through a slow ripening process during the region's long autumn. Inspired by their experiences in California's Napa Valley, owners Jane Langdon and Joe Will, who is also the award-winning winemaker, decided to make a cooking school part of the winery because, as Jane puts it, "food and wine go naturally together." Known for its award-winning Rieslings and Chardonnays, Strewn is also home to Terroir La Cachette, a pretty Provence-inspired dining room featuring the best of seasonal Niagara foods.

Pumpkin Praline Tart

The Waring House Inn, Picton
Makes 1 tart, approximately 8 servings

During the fall and into the festive season, pastry chef Marianne Sanders receives many requests for this recipe. Canned pumpkin purée is readily available in grocery stores, but it is particularly fresh around Thanksgiving and Christmas. Make sure to purchase the unsweetened type, with no seasonings already added. If you are pressed for time, use a pre-made, unbaked tart shell.

For the pastry:
1 ½ cups (375 mL) all-purpose flour
¼ tsp (1 mL) salt
⅛ tsp (.5 mL) baking powder
2–4 Tbsp (25–60 mL) ice water

⅔ cup (150 mL) unsalted butter, chilled
and cut into ½-inch (1.2-cm)
pieces

In a large mixing bowl, combine the flour, salt and baking powder. Add the chilled butter and, using a pastry cutter, work the butter into the flour mixture until the mixture resembles coarse meal. There should be no pieces larger than a pea. Sprinkle 2 Tbsp (25 mL) of the water over the flour and mix with a fork. Add more water if necessary, just enough so the dough holds together in a ball (the dough should not be sticky). Flatten dough into a disc and chill for 1 hour.

Preheat the oven to 375°F (180°C).

On a floured surface, roll out the dough to ⅛-inch (.3-cm) thickness. Press the dough into a 9-inch (23-cm) tart pan. Line with parchment paper and pie weights (or use dried beans or lentils), and bake for 10 minutes. Remove the parchment and weights and set aside to cool. Leave the oven on while preparing the filling.

For the filling:

3 eggs, at room temperature

¾ cup (175 mL) brown sugar

¼ cup (50 mL) granulated sugar

1 Tbsp (15 mL) molasses

2 cups (500 mL) pumpkin purée

1 Tbsp (15 mL) all-purpose flour

1 ½ tsp (7 mL) ground cinnamon

1 tsp (5 mL) ground ginger

¼ tsp (1 mL) ground nutmeg

¼ tsp (1 mL) ground cloves

¾ cup (175 mL) half-and-half cream

1 cup (250 mL) whipping cream

2 Tbsp (25 mL) brandy

In a large bowl, whisk together the eggs, sugars, molasses and pumpkin purée. Whisk in the flour, cinnamon, ginger, nutmeg and cloves. Finally, whisk in both the creams and the brandy. Pour the mixture into the cooled pie shell and bake for 45 minutes. While the pie is baking, prepare the praline topping.

For the topping:

⅓ cup (75 mL) butter

⅔ cup (150 mL) brown sugar

¼ cup (50 mL) whipping cream

½ cup (125 mL) pecans

½ cup (125 mL) walnuts

Heat the butter, sugar and cream in a small heavy saucepan. Bring to a boil and let boil for 3 minutes. Remove from heat and stir in the nuts.

Spoon the topping over the baked pie and slip under the broiler, about 3 inches (8 cm) from the heat. Broil until the topping is brown and bubbly. Allow to cool before serving.

Bittersweet Chocolate Waffles with Caramelized Bananas & Vanilla Rum Sauce

The Vintage Goose Inn and Spa, Kingsville
Makes 4 servings

Not just for breakfast or brunch, these homemade waffles are fine enough to star in this wonderful dessert. You'll need a waffle iron for this recipe.

For the waffles:
1 cup (250 mL) all-purpose flour

¼ cup (50 mL) cocoa powder

1 ¼ tsp (7 mL) baking powder

¼ tsp (1 mL) baking soda

pinch salt

2 ½ oz (75 g) semisweet chocolate, chopped

¼ cup (50 mL) granulated sugar

3 Tbsp (45 mL) butter

2 eggs

1 cup (250 mL) plus 2 Tbsp (15 mL) whole milk

1 ½ Tbsp (22 mL) Kirsch

¼ tsp (1 mL) pure vanilla extract

Sift the flour, cocoa powder, baking powder, soda and salt together in a large mixing bowl. Stir in the sugar. Set aside.

In a medium-sized heavy saucepan over low heat, melt the chocolate and butter. Remove from the heat and allow to cool slightly. Whisk in the eggs, milk, Kirsch and vanilla, and mix well.

Make a well in the dry ingredients and gradually whisk in the melted chocolate mixture.

Heat the waffle iron and make the waffles according to the manufacturer's instructions. Keep the waffles warm in a low oven while you finish the recipe.

For the caramelized bananas:

¼ cup (50 mL) butter

4 bananas, halved lengthwise, each half cut into 4 pieces

¼ cup (50 mL) brown sugar

⅓ cup (75 mL) dark rum

2 Tbsp (25 mL) water

1 fresh vanilla bean, finely chopped

½ tsp (2 mL) grated fresh nutmeg

½ tsp (2 mL) ground cinnamon

pinch salt

1 ¼ cups (300 mL) slivered almonds

In a heavy frying pan, melt the butter over high heat until the foam subsides, being careful not to allow the butter to burn. Add the bananas and sauté flat-side down, shaking the frying pan, for about 2 minutes. Remove the frying pan from the heat and sprinkle brown sugar around the bananas. Pour the rum over the bananas.

Return the frying pan to the heat and continue to sauté, shaking occasionally, about 2 more minutes. Add the water, vanilla, nutmeg, cinnamon and salt and cook over moderate heat until the sauce thickens, about another 3 minutes. Remove from the heat.

To serve, set 2 warm waffles on a serving plate and top with bananas. Drizzle the sauce over the waffles and sprinkle a few slivered almonds on top. Serve immediately.

Peach Cobbler

The Briars Resort & Spa, Jackson's Point
Recommended: Colio Estate Wines CEV Late Harvest Vidal
Makes 6 servings

An old-fashioned sweet that never fails to please. You will need six 6-oz (175-g) ramekins for this recipe. Serve these individual cobblers with a good-quality peach or butterscotch ripple ice cream.

For the filling:
3 cups (750 mL) peaches, peeled and diced

¼ cup (50 mL) brown sugar

¼ tsp (1 mL) ground cinnamon

¼ tsp (1 mL) ground nutmeg

¼ tsp (1 mL) ground cloves

¼ tsp (1 mL) allspice

¼ cup (50 mL) orange juice

2 tsp (10 mL) cornstarch mixed with 1 tsp (5 mL) water

Lightly grease the ramekins and set aside.

In a medium-sized heavy saucepan, combine the peaches, sugar, spices and orange juice. Bring to a boil and then reduce the heat to a simmer and cook for 3 minutes. Add the cornstarch mixture and simmer for a further 2 minutes, until the mixture thickens.

Fill each ramekin ¾ full with the peach mixture. Transfer to the refrigerator until needed.

For the topping:
½ cup (125 mL) all-purpose flour

¼ cup (50 mL) granulated sugar

¾ tsp (4 mL) baking powder

¼ tsp (1 mL) salt

1 Tbsp (15 mL) butter

1 Tbsp (15 mL) whipping cream

1 small egg, beaten

Mix the flour, sugar, baking powder and salt in a small bowl and set aside.

Heat the butter and cream in a medium-sized saucepan over low heat until the butter is just melted. Cool to room temperature.

Whisk the beaten egg into the butter mixture; add the dry ingredients and mix until combined. The mixture will resemble a thick pancake batter. Let rest for 10 minutes.

Preheat the oven to 350°F (180°C).

Spoon the batter over the peach filling, dividing it evenly between the 6 ramekins. Bake the cobblers for 25–30 minutes, until the topping is golden brown.

Serve immediately.

"Tea"ra Misu

HighFields Country Inn & Spa, Zephyr
Makes 4–6 servings

This is HighFields' twist on the traditional and very popular tiramisù. You'll need a candy thermometer for this recipe.

2 tsp (10 mL) unflavoured gelatin

2 Tbsp (25 mL) frozen orange juice
concentrate, thawed

½ cup (125 mL) granulated sugar

⅓ cup (75 mL) water

6 egg whites

½ cup (125 g) soft goat cheese

¾ cup (175 mL) goat's milk yogurt

½ tsp (2.5 mL) grated orange zest

½ tsp (2.5 mL) pure vanilla extract

2 packages ladyfingers, 3 ½ oz (85 g)
each

1 cup (250 mL) strong herbal tea
(orange or jasmine works well),
cooled

2 Tbsp (25 mL) cocoa powder

Warm the gelatin and orange juice concentrate in a small saucepan over low heat until the gelatin dissolves. Remove from the heat and set aside to cool.

In a medium-sized saucepan, combine the sugar and water. Cook over medium heat until the syrup reaches 234–240°F (112–116°C) on your candy thermometer.

In a medium-sized bowl, beat the egg whites until soft peaks form. Gradually add the syrup, beating constantly until the mixture is cool (this is called an Italian meringue). Beat in the gelatin mixture.

In a large bowl, beat together the cheese, yogurt, orange zest and vanilla. Fold in the meringue ⅓ at a time.

Separate the ladyfingers and line the bottom of a deep glass bowl or a 9- × 13-inch (3.5 L) baking pan with ½ the ladyfingers. Drizzle with ½ the tea. Cover with ½ the meringue mixture and ½ the cocoa. Repeat the layers. Refrigerate until set, about 4 hours. Serve chilled.

Apple Maple Soufflé

Ste. Anne's Country Inn & Spa, Grafton
Makes 6 servings

This can be held in the refrigerator unbaked for up to 6 hours, making it the perfect dessert for company. It is a particularly light soufflé as it uses no egg yolks. Save the yolks and use them in sauces, cakes, soups or stuffings.

8 egg whites
1 cup (250 mL) granulated sugar
3 Tbsp (45 mL) water
1 cup (250 mL) pure maple syrup

2 apples, peeled, cored, sliced and microwaved for 2 minutes until soft

Whip the egg whites with an electric mixer until soft to medium peaks are formed. Set aside.

Combine the sugar and water in a heavy saucepan. Bring to a boil over medium-high heat and continue boiling until the mixture thickens slightly and the bubbles begin to slow down.

Preheat the oven to 425°F (220°C). Add the maple syrup and apples to the sugar mixture. Cook over medium heat for about 5 minutes. Remove from the heat.

Give the egg whites another beating and slowly add the hot syrup mixture to them, folding the egg whites around the syrup mixture. When the mixture has cooled to warm (not hot), spoon into ovenproof ceramic or glass ramekins. (At this point the soufflé can be refrigerated for up to 6 hours.) Bake for 10 minutes until the soufflés are puffed and brown. Serve immediately.

Pecan Bourbon Pie

The Merrill Inn, Picton
Makes 8 servings

This sumptuous pie speaks with a decidedly southern accent thanks to the pecans and bourbon. Be sure to leave the oven on after baking the pie shell; the filled shell will bake at the same temperature. Also, note that if using a deep pie pan, the filling may take longer to cook.

For the sweet dough:

⅓ cup (75 mL) butter

¼ cup (50 mL) granulated sugar

1 small egg, beaten

⅔ cup (150 mL) all-purpose flour

Cream the butter and sugar together in a large bowl. Mix in the beaten egg. Add the flour all at once and gently combine without overworking the dough. Shape into a disc, wrap in plastic wrap and refrigerate for 2 hours.

Preheat the oven to 350°F (180°C).

Roll out the dough to ¼-inch (0.5 cm) thickness on a floured surface and place in a 10-inch (25-cm) fluted flan dish or pie dish. Line the pastry with parchment paper and pie weights (or use dried beans or lentils) and blind-bake for 10 minutes. Remove the parchment and weights and bake for a further 10 minutes. Allow the shell to cool completely on a rack while preparing the filling.

For the filling:

3 eggs

1 cup (250 mL) granulated sugar

⅓ cup (75 mL) butter, melted and
  cooled

1 cup (250 mL) corn syrup

2 Tbsp (25 mL) bourbon

1 ½ cups (375 mL) pecan halves

Beat the eggs and sugar together in a large bowl. Slowly whisk in the melted butter. Add the corn syrup and bourbon and stir well to combine.

Place the pecan halves in the baked and cooled pie shell. Use enough to cover the bottom, but not more than a single layer. Gently pour the filling over the pecans and stir to evenly distribute the pecans.

Bake for 30–35 minutes, until the centre is set when gently shaken. Cool before serving.

Fig Tart with Red Wine Syrup

The Inn at Manitou, McKellar
Makes 4

With a little help from frozen puff pastry, this stylish recipe is a breeze to pull together. Start by making the red wine syrup. For a nice variation on this theme, place slices of goat cheese atop the figs before baking.

For the syrup:

1 ½ cups (375 mL) dry red wine

¼ cup (50 mL) granulated sugar

½ cinnamon stick

½ vanilla bean

grated zest of 1 orange

grated zest of 1 lemon

Combine all the ingredients in a saucepan. Bring to a boil and cook gently until reduced to a syrup-like consistency, about 15–20 minutes. Strain through a sieve, discard the solids and set the syrup to one side.

For the tarts:

14 oz (398-g) pkg. frozen puff pastry, thawed

3 Tbsp (45 mL) granulated sugar

1 tsp (5 mL) ground cinnamon

4 fresh figs (preferably black), halved

Preheat the oven to 400°F (200°C).

Roll out the puff pastry and, using a 6-inch (15-cm) pastry cutter, cut out 4 rounds. Spray a baking sheet with a little cooking spray (or lightly butter) and transfer the rounds of pastry to it. In a little bowl, combine the sugar and cinnamon and blend well. Sprinkle a bit of this mixture over the surface of the pastry rounds. Arrange 2 fig halves on top of each pastry round, followed by more of the sugar-cinnamon mixture. Bake in the oven for about 20 minutes or until the pastry is golden and puffed. Let sit for a minute or 2 before serving with the barely warm syrup.

Chocolate Pâte

The Hillcrest, A Valenova Inn & Spa, Port Hope
Makes 6 servings

At last—a rich chocolate dessert that's truly low-fat and delicious. The orange juice and zest give a wonderful lift to the chocolate's intensity. The yogurt needs to drain overnight to thicken and the finished preparation needs at least 4 hours to chill, so be sure to begin a day and a half ahead. Serve with fresh berries and whipped cream, if desired.

3 cups (750 mL) low-fat plain yogurt
6 oz (175 g) bittersweet chocolate
1 cup (250 mL) freshly squeezed
   orange juice, chilled

1 Tbsp (15 mL) grated orange zest
½ envelope unflavoured gelatin
   powder

Pour the yogurt into a strainer lined with cheesecloth and suspend over a large bowl. Cover with plastic wrap and place in the refrigerator overnight. The following day the yogurt will have the consistency of light cream cheese. Remove the strained yogurt to a large mixing bowl. Discard the liquid that has collected in the bowl.

Melt the chocolate over simmering water in a double boiler. Set aside.

Combine the orange juice, zest and gelatin powder in a small saucepan. Place over medium heat until warm. Slowly add the orange juice mixture to the yogurt, mixing well until blended. Fold in the melted chocolate.

Generously spray a loaf pan with a non-stick cooking spray. Pour the mixture into the pan and tap the pan on the counter top until the mixture is level. Cover tightly with plastic wrap and refrigerate 4 hours or overnight.

Release the pâte from the pan by placing the bottom of the pan in warm water for 30 seconds. Slide a knife around the inside of all 4 sides of the pan. Turn the pan upside down onto a cutting board. Tap the bottom and sides of the pan and the pâte will slide out.

Slice and serve on individual plates.

Index

About the Authors

Kathleen Sloan-McIntosh has been writing about food and drink for newspapers and magazines for 25 years and is the author of seven cookbooks, including two that have garnered Silver Cuisine Canada Awards—*The Sticks & Stones Cookbook* and *A Year in Niagara: the People and Food of Wine Country*. She lives in Bayfield, Ontario, where she and her husband are the proud owners of The Black Dog Village Pub & Bistro.

Kathleen's daughter, Jenna C. King, has been a freelance writer for 10 years, and her recipes have appeared in numerous cookbooks, including *Rustic Italian Cooking, A Year in Niagara* and *New Celtic Cooking*. Jenna lives in Toronto with her partner and their nine-year-old son. When her son was born, Jenna started her own baking business, specializing in custom-made cakes, pies, tarts and cookies. She is currently studying at the University of Toronto and working as a part-time administrative assistant at Avalon, one of Toronto's best restaurants.

Together, this mother and daughter cooking and writing team present *Simply the Best: Food and Wine from Ontario's Finest Inns*, a culinary journey through the best of Ontario hospitality.